WALKED ON

BRIAN KENT

WALKED ON

LIFE LESSONS FROM A TWO-SPORT
NON-SCHOLARSHIP COLLEGE ATHLETE

BRIAN KENT

First Edition
Printed in the United States of America
ISBN: 978-1-7360903-1-2

BKSTRENGTH.COM

DEDICATION

This book is dedicated to my family, friends, teammates, coaches, clients, and training partners. Thank you for understanding my process and for being a part of the journey.

In loving memory of my grandfather, Irving Marshak (1922-2018). Irv never missed any of my T-Ball, Little League, Pee Wee football, YMCA basketball, or South football and baseball games. He traveled everywhere — whether I was playing or sitting on the bench. Once in Iowa City, Irv parked his Buick LeSabre in a spot reserved for head football coach Hayden Fry. True story.

TABLE OF CONTENTS

Coach Kent reminding his running backs that we're always one play away from a touchdown. With Dan Stringfellow. Photo by Dick Cook

FOREWORD

I was very privileged to coach Brian in both football and baseball on the youth and high school levels. As a youth coach I hope that I gave him the impression that everyone plays and everyone sits the bench. My philosophy was to teach the kids how to play the game through fundamentals and teamwork, and have fun while we do it. Everyone matters and everyone plays. I hope that my love of both games carried over to the team members. I also had to wear two different hats, as my answer to "how did I do today" was very different from Coach or Dad. I have passed that bit of advice to many other dads who have coached their sons and they have all appreciated it. Brian didn't get it at the time, but he now understands the difference.

Brian accurately describes his years playing football and baseball at Downers Grove South. The challenge for me was separating my dad persona from my coach persona. I have always taken the responsibility of being a father and a high school coach very seriously. I believe that coaches should serve as role models and act accordingly. Brian was very fortunate to have had many excellent high school coaches. We stressed that hard work and preparation can overcome just about anything.

Unfortunately, later in life, Brian discovered that hard work does not guarantee success, but we certainly stressed that in football. At South, no one outworked us or was better prepared for an opponent.

Sometimes Brian took the hard work mantra to the extreme. The summer before his senior year in high school saw him practicing football from 6:30 to 10 every morning and catching double headers every afternoon. After his senior year he overtrained to prepare for Iowa. This overtraining led to the mononucleosis that began his collegiate career. I tried to get him to take days off, but at the time, he did not understand the need for rest and recovery. I'm sure he does now.

I have coached high school football for more than 40 years, baseball for 12. One of my greatest joys in life is to have been able to coach my son. I hope that I was able to instill in Brian the work ethic needed to be successful. My wife, Juli, and I have encouraged him to write this book for many years. As a parent one can only to hope to raise your children the right way and give them the tools to become independent thinkers and live their own lives.

I believe the book is a very accurate recounting of the trials and tribulations in Brian's athletic career. One of the few bits of advice he ignored was to concentrate on baseball, because he was better at it — but he enjoyed playing football more. I can't tell you the thrill I got traveling to Tucson with my brother to watch Brian practice and play with the White Sox organization. I may be a Cubs fan, but I will never hate the White Sox for giving him the opportunity, his dream, his chance. Isn't that what we all want — a chance to live out our dream?

Enjoy the book.

—

TERRY KENT

Illinois High School Football Coaches Association Hall Of Fame: 2010

Illinois High School Baseball Coaches Association Assistant Coach Of The Year: 2006

ALFAC National Assistant Football Coach Of The Year: 2002

Football State Champion, 8A: 2001

Photo by Nolis Anderson

INTRO

"OH, THE PLACES YOU'LL GO."
– Dr. Seuss

My name is Brian Kent, and I am a Chicago-based, self-employed personal trainer. I am also part of the leadership council at On Your Mark Coaching and Training and a Nike trainer. As a writer, I have written for the National Academy of Sports Medicine (NASM) and STACK Magazine, as well as numerous blogs for my website, bkstrength.com. Prior to becoming a trainer, I was a football player at the University of Iowa, a baseball player at the University of Nebraska, and a minor league baseball player, finishing my career with the Chicago White Sox organization. A lifelong martial artist, I am a black belt in taekwondo, a black belt in judo, and as of this writing, a purple belt in Brazilian jiu-jitsu.

While the previous paragraph is all true, my journey to find athletic success was extremely difficult. Keep in mind that "difficult" is personally defined; what is difficult for one may not be considered difficult for another. We all have to face and overcome our own version of adversity, as my journey as an athlete was the opposite of easy (please keep my struggle in perspective, because plenty of people have had worse problems and harder situations than mine). I am fortunate to come from a supportive family and grew up with excellent youth and high school coaches, teaching me great life lessons. But, once I got to college, none of that mattered.

What I learned on the field in the first 18 years of my life was no longer relevant.

Before becoming a trainer, I was an athlete. In high school, I had big dreams: I wanted to play Big Ten football *and* Major League Baseball. These were high-level aspirations, and the statistics work against most high school players achieving either of them. In fact, according to scholarshipstats.com, only 1 in 14 high school athletes will play a varsity college sport; and only 1 in 54 will play an NCAA Division I sport; about 2 percent of high school athletes will earn a Division I athletic scholarship; and 2 percent of the high school athletes that earn Division I scholarships will play professionally. The math was against me. I knew it would be hard, but I was convinced that I could do it. While I would not have been able to articulate it at the time, I believed in me. There was something deep inside my core that "wanted it more" than everyone else. As cliché as it sounds, I believed anything was possible if I had talent, worked hard, made sacrifices, and was willing to go through hell to get it. I accepted that suffering was a component of achievement, and I was willing to suffer. I did not expect it to be easy.

The journey was made all the more difficult without the validation of personal recognition. I did not receive many individual awards. As a high school athlete, I was All-Conference for football and baseball, All-Area for football and baseball, and played in an All-Star football game. But, unlike many pro athletes, I was not All-State and I was not an All-American. I was not offered a Division I college football or baseball scholarship. I was not drafted by an MLB team out of high school or college. The reality of my background is that I was a two sport walk-on and an undrafted free agent.

Being a walk-on meant that no college football or college baseball program thought enough of my potential to pay for my education. Being an undrafted free agent meant that no Major League Baseball organizations thought enough of my potential to draft me. I wore the walk-on and undrafted free agent designation like a chip on my shoulder — as a motivator. The odds are against walk-ons succeeding, as we are presumed to be less talented than our scholarship peers. Thus, there are fewer opportunities to show what we can do. Somehow, we *must* find a way to stand out. Being in the right place at the right time, and ready to perform when called upon is important. Focusing on controllable actions, such as preparation, is a must. Preparation is an equalizer, so being ready is better than getting ready.

As an athlete with an English degree, I had zero interest in writing about my sports career, but as I've gotten older, my attitude about it has changed. There are very few people that know the in-depth details of this story. As a trainer, I have worked with athletes and been disgusted after hearing about their experiences with college coaches, which sounded very similar to my experiences with college coaches. After realizing that 2017 marked the 10th anniversary of my release from the Chicago White Sox organization, I felt I was removed enough from the game to offer my own insights.

Reading a book like this would have helped reinforce my belief that I was on the right path. There were many sleepless nights wondering if I would ever achieve the goals that I had set for myself. I hope that my persistence motivates someone else to keep fighting for what they want. Staying true to my core beliefs helped me navigate through the shit-storm that is college and professional sports.

* * * *

Walked On is organized so that each chapter represents specific sequencing on my timeline. Chapters are listed as the order of operations dictates, from earliest events to most recent. Much of what happened occurred within the past 20 years, so I understand there may be skepticism regarding my memory's accuracy. But, I wrote college essays about these experiences while they were happening — papers that I still have and used for reference. From my perspective, the evidence and my memory are a match. The LINCOLN and OMAHA chapters were extremely difficult to write, as I had to relive years of anger and frustration. Private memories that had been locked away — memories that I am not proud of — are now accessible for all to read. The blueprint of this book has been in my brain for years. After a freak judo accident, I had ankle surgery in November, 2017. I was in a non-weight bearing boot for six weeks, and not able to train clients. To make myself productive while on the "Disabled List," I sat at the computer and organized my thoughts. Fueled by numerous glasses of Bulleit Bourbon and continuous physical adjustments to elevate my leg, I bit down on my figurative mouthpiece and cranked out multiple revisions of this story. (If Bruce Lee could famously write *Tao of Jeet Kune Do* after injuring his back, then I could write *Walked On* after injuring my ankle.) The following chapters are written from my perspective about real events. Everything you read actually happened.

Not every decision I made throughout this journey was correct. All athletes are at the mercy of other people's opinions, and coaching actions forced my reactions. It is important to note that, regardless of my experiences, I am a happy person and extremely fulfilled. I have a great family, an inspired career, and an amazing life. This book was written out of enlightenment and reflection, to connect with future athletic audiences. *Walked On* is an attempt to explain some unfortunate realities of big-time college and professional sports; a demonstration to current and future athletes that success can be determined by our inner strength. This book has many characters, including family, teammates, and coaches. They all have important roles in the story; some as heroes, others as villains — some as both.

Let it be known that I hold no grudges and wish the heroes and villains a lifetime of success and prosperity.

The purpose of this writing is to use my own journey to motivate others to find inspiration through failure and setbacks. I am well aware that if I had an easier athletic path (for example, if I had been All-State, if I had received a scholarship, if I had been drafted) then my journey would have been completely different. Maybe, in a crazy alternate universe, my life would be forever changed if opportunities were handed to me. Maybe I would have lost focus, maybe I would have gotten lazy, maybe I would have settled for shortcuts. Or maybe this story would be about my amazing college football career plus a decade of big league service time...

Either way, at a pivotal point we are all tested on how bad we want something. During a life-defining moment, we must decide that our personal grit outweighs any obstacle. We must believe that our ability to fight is greater than our instinct to run; that our will can overcome our challenge. My hope is that this book provides numerous examples of times it would have been easy to quit, but a commitment to achieving a life-long goal and the resiliency to see it through proved to be more important. I refused to let any single opinion define me; the only opinion that mattered was mine.

Special thanks to my family for their support. They lived through each chapter and always picked up the phone when I called.

Photos by Dick Cook

SOUTH

"NOBODY WHO EVER GAVE THEIR BEST REGRETTED IT."

– George S Halas

I grew up a block away from Downers Grove South High School, located near 63rd Street in Downers Grove, Illinois. South (as we referred to it) is a public, middle-class neighborhood high school about 20 miles southwest of Chicago. South has been in the Kent family for many years. From 1987-2017, my dad, Terry, was a math teacher and a football, wrestling, and baseball coach. I graduated in 1997, my sister Maggie in 2006, and my youngest sister Ally in 2008. My mom, Juli, spent a million hours going to football games and baseball games all across Chicagoland. Our family calendar revolved around our separate, yet overlapping, South schedules.

At the time, South had an enrollment of about 3,200, making it one of the largest single-building high schools in Illinois. The student body came primarily from neighboring Downers Grove and Woodridge, and it was a diverse group. There were kids that went off to the Ivy League; others that didn't graduate (according to Wikipedia, the average ACT score is

22). I loved South, but as students, we endured some violent tragedies during my four years. Freshman year, a student was shot and killed during a varsity football game. Sophomore year, a horrific car accident involving several football players instantly killed wide receiver Antoine Mangram. Junior year, All-State basketball player Antwaun Cubie murdered Jeremy Bruder — my neighbor — over a drug deal gone wrong. Senior year, Brent Cobb was killed trying to playfully jump off a train that had left downtown Chicago. While Downers Grove is generally a safe neighborhood, some crazy shit happened at South during my time there. We had to deal with real-life scenarios that probably made us mature a little bit faster.

While John Hughes's movies offered one depiction of the suburban Chicago high school experience, our environment made us different. With so many kids in one building, conflict was inevitable. Throughout his career, Terry broke up numerous fights by his third floor classroom. South had both a Behavioral Disorder department and an English as a Second Language program, plus an armed police officer in school at all times, which was rare for the area. The diversity gave us a glimpse into real-world living and a view into the daily struggles of students from various backgrounds. We had to learn how to coexist. From a sports perspective, it was essential that we set aside our individual differences and find ways to work together to benefit the team.

* * * *

I was excited and proud to be part of the football program. South football was extremely disciplined, almost militant. We were not allowed to smoke cigarettes or drink alcohol, and our hair was always to be kept short. The program had a "no earring policy" as well, and any violation of these rules resulted in immediate removal from the team. South football players had a choice: Follow the code and be part of the program, or don't play football. It was expected that we answered questions with *Yes* or *Yes sir*. Responding with *Yeah* was for undisciplined teams and unacceptable, resulting in punishment sprints after practice. We were taught that discipline was the foundation of our success, and we were successful. A total commitment to the program was expected, along with being a beast between the lines and a gentleman off the field. Going into my senior year, South had 12 consecutive conference championships and playoff appearances, always competing against the largest schools in Chicagoland. In 1984 and 1993 we lost in the state finals. In 2001, we beat the #4 team *in the country* to become 8A State Champions. Tradition never graduates.

One of the main reasons for our success was the outstanding coaching staff. Head coach John Belskis and assistants Tim Mash, Jack McInerney, Terry McCombs, and my dad would all eventually be inducted into the Illinois High School Football Coaches Hall of Fame. All of Coach Belskis's assistants had been varsity head coaches somewhere else, and they were a tight group. Some schools were lucky if they had a single Hall of Fame coach — South had five! We were always prepared and knew what our opponents would do before they did it.

We had the most experienced group of high school football coaches in Chicagoland, and our practice schedule was structured around the opposing team's scouting report. South taught us how to prepare and how to practice; every detail was important. We were never out-coached.

I started playing Pee Wee football when I was 9 years-old, and our Downers Grove Panthers travel teams were pretty good. As a kid, I primarily played defense as an outside linebacker. I liked tackling people but really wanted to play offense and score touchdowns. Fullback was my favorite position. I loved everything that fullbacks represented and there was something special about leading the way on every play and smashing into defenders. To me, fullbacks were the "tough guys" and set the tone for the entire team. When I got to South, fullback was the only position that I wanted to play. I achieved my individual goals of being the starting fullback on the freshman and sophomore teams, but as a junior, I found myself on the varsity bench.

The senior Class of 1996 had been undefeated as underclassmen and through three seasons, had a 29-1 overall high school record. Many of my fellow juniors quit football, realizing that they were buried on the depth chart behind senior talent. Going into the 1995 season, incumbent seniors occupied 19 of the 22 combined offensive and defensive starting positions, and their reputation was well-known. The *Chicago Tribune* ranked us as the preseason No. 1 team in Illinois. I understood why the seniors had priority but prepared myself like I was the starter.

One consistent message the coaches drilled into us — a message that I still believe in — was that at some point, whether in practice or in the game (or in life), we would be given an opportunity to prove ourselves. If we make the most of this opportunity, we will be rewarded with more opportunities. So, all that we can control is our focus and preparation. We must be patient, and wait for our number to be called. When our number is called, it's time to step up and get the job done.

Our season opening game was against Stevenson High School; it's a long drive from South to northwest suburban Lincolnshire. We had knocked them out of the playoffs the previous year, and knew they would be hunting for revenge and our coveted, No. 1 ranking. They jumped on us early and by the time I entered the game, the massacre was about over; we were losing by four touchdowns in the fourth quarter. Still, it was a chance for me to prove myself as a varsity player. I caught a fourth down pass for a first down to extend a drive; blocked two guys on Terry Mitchell's long touchdown run; and scored my first varsity touchdown. We lost 35-21, which sucked, but I played well and made the most of my opportunity.

I was rewarded. After the loss to Stevenson, the coaches adjusted our ineffective lineup and I was promoted to the starting fullback. In Week 2 at Oak Park River Forest, I was involved in a collision that fast-tracked my athletic career. We had a play-action pass called "Sucker Pass" that only worked because returning senior tailback Dan Stringfellow was a proven threat. Stringfellow had speed and demanded attention, so a fake handoff and some pulling lineman would "sucker" the defense into believing that he had the ball, and I was left all alone to sneak out of the backfield, catch a pass, and run.

Quarterback Gregg Richards' pass hit me right between the fours on my #44 jersey, and as I ran up the field an Oak Park defensive back finally stepped up to make the tackle. With a full head of steam, I had two choices: Go around him, or go through him. I decided I would channel my inner Walter Payton — my favorite football player of all time — and go through him. I lowered my shoulder to initiate the contact, and upon impact, knew I was the hammer and not the nail. The crowd's reaction confirmed it. My teammates would later say the collision sounded like an on-field car accident. The game film showed me running through my opponent, followed by the offense and our sideline celebrating a big hit, while he lay motionless on the ground. The defender had to be carried off the field, as I cracked his face mask and broken his nose. We won the game; I ran for a touchdown and caught a pass for a 2-point conversion. I also established myself as a big hitter and an impact player.

The following week at Willowbrook, with everyone still keying on Stringfellow, I took a handoff up the middle and broke into the second-level of their defense. I was met in the secondary by the free safety, who was also their quarterback. We violently collided. Again, I was the hammer. I jumped up to celebrate another big hit, but he stayed down and needed to be carried off the field. In two weeks, I had knocked two players out of the game, and we had two wins. After the Willowbrook game, my name was in the Preps Plus section of the *Tribune*. I had started the season on the bench, but quickly became a weapon — the result of taking advantage of an opportunity. Over the next two years, I never left the offensive huddle and was a team captain as a senior. College recruiters began to take notice after my junior season when I averaged 7.0 yards per carry, could catch the ball out of the backfield, and was a punishing blocker.

*　　*　　*　　*

After losing in the second round of the 1995 playoffs, I was back in the South weight room two days later. The weight room, located in the school's indoor track, was basement level and not visually appealing: no windows, an old, cage-like fence surrounded the perimeter, and years of sweat stains were caked on the concrete floor. Sometimes the radio worked, most times it didn't. Aesthetics aside, it was a place to build champions. Back then, we had the typical racks and platforms for football-themed lifts. We also had many, very old and dusty Nautilus multi-station machines (gym teachers teased that they were donated from the prison in nearby Joliet). Aside from baseball season, I trained everyday from November until football camp started in June. The thought of anyone in Chicagoland working harder than me — or wanting it more than me — made me sick to my stomach. What I should have realized was that working smarter is better than working harder. In addition to following the mandatory South football strength and conditioning program, I ran the sledding hill at O'Brien Park. I pushed the Kent family Ford Escort across the South parking lot. I ran the Mustang Stadium steps. No one told me to do it, it was all intrinsic motivation. This was the era before personal trainers and specialized coaches; kids either inspired themselves or they didn't. With the help of a Rage Against The Machine and 2Pac mixtape blasting from my Sony Walkman headphones, I could lead myself into deep discomfort. While the organization of my training was poor, and recovery was nonexistent, the effort and desire was maximum. It was a theme that both helped and hurt me in the future.

Through the South football program, I learned the importance of being the first person to arrive and the last one to leave. During summer camp, as a team, we would often jog four blocks to O'Brien Park, sprint ten times up the sledding hill, then jog back to school. I would finish my sprints and keep running the hill until all my teammates were through, often doing double to triple the work. I wanted my legs to be so strong that no one could tackle me one-on-one. If some hill sprints were good, then more were definitely better. Besides, every Chicago Bears fan knew that Walter Payton took his conditioning to elite levels by running hills, so if hill-running was good enough for Sweetness, then it was good enough for me.

While South had years of success, we rarely had Division I talent. But, we did have Mike McGrath. Mike was in the class of 1995, twice an All-State free safety, and a scholarship player at Indiana University. The late, iconic ABC announcer Keith Jackson once described Mike as a "thumper" during a nationally televised Big Ten broadcast. Mike was a big hitter and I wanted to be like Mike. I also hoped to achieve some personal success like Mike. During my junior year, I thought there was a chance I could be voted All-Conference. I wasn't. As I sat in the Kent kitchen, eating breakfast and looking through the *Tribune* sports section at all the All-Conference and All-State names that didn't include mine, Terry could sense my disappointment. Our conversation went something like this:

Dad: Do you think you should have been All-Conference?
Me: Yes.
Dad: Do you still think you're one of the best players?
Me: Yes.
Dad: Do you really need a piece of paper to tell you that you're the best?
Me: No.
Dad: Then keep doing what you're doing.

To this day it is the best piece of advice I have ever received. However, I still ripped out the All-State teams from the *Chicago Tribune* and *Chicago Sun-Times* and highlighted all the juniors that made it instead of me. I taped it to the back of my bedroom door, and if I ever lacked motivation, then all I needed to do was glance at the door and the fire was re-lit.

*   *   *   *

South baseball was a completely different experience. Unlike football, baseball was a struggling program. We lost more than we won, and we were not a dominant force in our conference or the state. Baseball did not have football's level of discipline, reflected in some players earrings and long hair. At football practice, Coach Belskis enforced an elitism culture that chastised less-disciplined schools, saying, "If you want to have long hair and earrings go to Downers Grove *North*." This was an example of the stark contrast between the two programs. Football had discipline and success; baseball had less discipline and less success. While football and baseball are completely different sports, attracting different types of athletes, I struggled internally over which way was the "right way."

Rudy Boker was the varsity baseball head coach and my freshman PE teacher. Once, during our track and field unit, Coach Boker asked for a volunteer to run the 400m-dash. Wanting to impress him, I stepped up. I had never run a 400m-dash before, nor did I know how far 400m was. But, I was ready to make the most of this opportunity and display my (lack of) speed. As a "ball athlete," I knew absolutely nothing about track distances. After the first 100m, I realized this was a mistake. I had never sprinted one lap around the track before, and my legs and lungs were dead. Not wanting to quit, I pushed it until the end. I looked and sounded like Homer Simpson as I crossed the finish line, vomiting all over the track. I exhausted every ounce of energy and started to lose consciousness so Coach Boker mercifully sent me to the nurse's office for the rest of class. *Thanks coach.*

Today, with the rise of travel teams, kids are playing more structured baseball year-round. But, back then, high school baseball was the first time teenagers consistently played on real-sized fields. The dimensions of high school infields are the same as Wrigley Field or Comiskey Park — the bases are 90 feet apart. There were plenty of players who were great in Little League that got cut from their high school teams, because Little League curve balls are ineffective from 60 feet 6 inches.

I had been a catcher since 9 years-old, and loved everything about the position. The "tools of ignorance" distinguished me from every other player on the field, and I was attracted to the art of gearing up for battle. Equally appealing was the leadership aspect of catching: game-planning each pitch, positioning the defense, managing umpire relationships, and the psychology of working with my pitcher. Catching is the most demanding position in all of sports, but spending the whole game in a deep squat was quite comfortable for me. In Little League, my grandfather, Irv, used to sit behind the backstop and offer advice through the fence. Any time a pitch got past me, I would have to turn around and hustle toward him to retrieve it. Meanwhile, we'd lock eyes and he'd loudly remind me to "KEEP YOUR EYE ON THE BALL" or to "WATCH THE BALL." I didn't like hearing his voice, but understood that if I played better and kept everything in front of me, Irv would stay quiet.

Terry had also been a catcher and helped build my foundation. He taught me the fundamentals of receiving pitches, blocking balls in the dirt, and how clean footwork correlated to accurate throwing. Over the years, I developed consistency throwing the ball — on a line — across the diamond. As my body matured and middle school clumsiness morphed into high school athleticism, I could maintain balance from my crouch and became a solid defensive catcher. Coach Boker must have been impressed by either my catching ability or my 400m-dash effort, because he promoted me to the varsity midway through my sophomore year. With South being such a large school, it was rare for any underclassmen to play a varsity sport. On my 16th birthday, I made my debut and was the worst player on the field. I struck out three times and had terrible defense. Baseball is notorious for humbling the overconfident, and I squandered my varsity opportunity.

* * * *

I was certain Coach Boker had seen enough, that I had played my way to a demotion. Hell, I would have sent my ass back to the sophomore squad. For a reason I will never understand, he stuck with me and kept me in the lineup. The 1995 team finished the regular season with a .500 record, but caught fire in the playoffs. I was our starting catcher. We were Regional Champions for the first time since 1988 and one win away from being Sectional Champions. Winning the Sectional was a ticket to the State Finals, a place no South baseball team had ever been before. All we had to do was beat Morris High School.

Morris was 34-4 and one of the top teams in the state; we were 18-15, and somehow winning games that, on paper, we should have lost. Somebody was going to State. The game

with Morris is one I will remember forever. The bleachers at host Oswego High School were packed, and it was a hostile crowd. It was the first time I had ever been heckled, and the Morris fans were all over me. If their game-plan was to rattle the sophomore catcher, it worked. I heard everything they said and had a hard time concentrating. The game was close, and behind the plate, the stress made my butthole tighter and tighter. In the late innings with the score tied, Morris had a baserunner on second with two outs. As he attempted to steal third, a good throw by me would have ended the inning. However, my throw bounced past third baseman Andrew LeCrone and skipped into left field, allowing the go-ahead run to score. The Morris crowd went into a frenzy and continued to taunt me.

We never recovered and lost the Sectional Championship by one run — a run that scored on my throwing error. I was convinced my mistake ended our season and apologized to all the seniors. Coach Boker retired after the game. But, my performance against Morris fueled me to never have that feeling again. I was determined to play well under pressure and stay in control of my emotions. I needed to keep the game simple and block out distractions. As a future three-year varsity starter, and two-season captain, it was my job to provide leadership. Leaders must keep their focus under all conditions, they can't cry in the dugout when they lose.

Phil Fox took over for Boker before my junior year. Coach Fox had also been my sophomore football coach, so I knew and liked him. He asked my dad to join him on the varsity staff. Coach Fox would soon make his way into the Illinois High School Baseball Coaches Association Hall of Fame, and eventually be employed by the Chicago Bulls/Sox Academy, running baseball clinics for kids. Terry would later be named the Assistant Coach of the Year by the IHSBCA. As in football, I was extremely lucky to be the beneficiary of such a talented high school coaching staff. Although my offense was nonexistent as a sophomore, I hit .333 as a junior and .402 as a senior, and from a preparation standpoint, I was as ready for college as anyone could be.

South baseball did not have a Mike McGrath, or any lineage of Division I ballplayers. Bobby Daly was drafted by the New York Mets in 1992, and the aforementioned Andrew LeCrone was drafted by the Florida Marlins in 1995. Daly played four years in the Mets system, while LeCrone turned down the Marlins in favor of his football scholarship to the University of Tulsa. Unless I was drafted, there was no college baseball blueprint to follow. As a graduate in the Class of 1997, I had to do it my own way.

Jersey photos taken with my Sun Bowl-issued disposable camera.
Photos by Brian Kent

IOWA CITY

**"IT'S NOT WHETHER YOU GET KNOCKED DOWN,
IT'S WHETHER YOU GET UP."**

– Vince Lombardi

A successful high school career at South fueled my confidence that I could compete at the highest Division I collegiate levels. My logic dictated that if I could perform well at a large high school, then I could perform well at a large college. We played against a dozen Division I athletes, so I saw what those types of bodies look like: big, strong, and fast. I had no fear meeting them head on. I liked to compete and wanted to test myself against the best in the country. While I had some size and some skill, I was not the biggest, strongest, or fastest player on any field. My recruitable assets were probably mentality and athleticism. On the gridiron, I quickly memorized our football playbook and always knew what my job was. On the diamond, I was extremely accountable and liked being in a leadership position. Besides, I was a two-sport team captain at one of the biggest high schools in Illinois, so scholarship or not, I knew there was a place for me. *Do you really need a piece of paper to tell you you're the best?* But, I wasn't sure where or for which sport. With football, I spent endless hours watching game footage and preparing my personal VHS highlight tape, which I packaged and mailed to every school in the Big Ten Conference. For baseball, as a left-handed hitting catcher, I hoped there would be equal interest. In a perfect world, I would stay close to home and play in the Big Ten. Besides, the Big Ten loved Chicagoland fullbacks. Chris Gall was at Indiana (Oak Park River Forest), Cecil Martin was at Wisconsin (Evanston), Demetrius Smith was at Michigan (Richards), and Mike Alstott was at Purdue (Joliet Catholic). I was ready to join the club.

My physical size hurt me for football yet helped me for baseball. As a lean 6'2" and 200-ish pounds, I was considered a small and slow fullback; but a big and fast catcher. (From a speed perspective, my best 40-yard dash time was 4.94 and my best 60-yard dash time was 7.19. I was competitive, but never a burner. However, I always felt that I played faster in the chaos of a real game with intangibles that no stopwatch could measure.) Different sports have different positional requirements, and I was caught between these two worlds. Many college recruiters look for specific body-types and try to predict a player's development under their program's influence. With height, big legs and a big ass, I was thought to have the "frame" to add 20-30 pounds on my college-athlete-body. While I was too small and too slow to immediately contribute in the Big Ten, Coach Belskis thought I was talented enough to compete after getting bigger, stronger, and faster. Coach Fox thought I would have success catching for any Division I school. Their belief in me reinforced my confidence.

Throughout the recruiting process, I was constantly asked which sport I liked better. The real answer was that in the fall I liked football better, and in the spring I liked baseball better. In the winter and summer I liked them equally. But, I put myself at a disadvantage by endorsing both sports. My love of football scared off baseball scouts; my love of baseball scared off football coaches. I wanted to play two sports and thought I was good enough to be like Bo Jackson and Deion Sanders. Hell, if they could play both sports, why couldn't I? I was willing to put in the work and make sacrifices, so why not me?

Then, like now, college football ruled the college sports kingdom. It was on TV every Saturday and on my mind all the time. College baseball had zero presence. It wasn't covered by the Chicago newspapers, wasn't written about in *Sports Illustrated*, and wasn't on TV. Aside from the College World Series, it was almost as if college baseball didn't exist. College football gave paid-in-full scholarships, while college baseball gave yearly-renewable-partial scholarships. From an attraction standpoint, college football resembled Jenny McCarthy while college baseball was the Invisible Woman.

I received Division I attention in both sports, but no scholarship offers (Division II Hillsdale College (MI) offered me a partial football scholarship, but the private tuition was still too expensive, so I politely declined). Some football schools invited me to walk-on. A few wanted me to play middle linebacker — a position I had never played before. Meanwhile, there were no baseball scholarship offers either.

Selecting a college and a college sport became increasingly difficult and stressful. I assumed someone would offer me, and I would accept. But, it wasn't happening.

*   *   *   *

The University of Iowa football program, led by legendary coach Hayden Fry, was known for poaching loads of Chicago talent. Coach Fry built his teams with a core of Iowans, Texans, and Chicagoans. Iowa also had a highly respected walk-on program, with a reputation for treating all players equally. Former Iowa standout quarterback Chuck Long, then a coach on Fry's staff, was in charge of recruiting in Chicago. Iowa had been contacting me since my junior year, but Coach Long was clear that fullback was not usually a scholarship position. Instead, he offered me a roster spot as a preferred walk-on. Coach Long explained that Iowa only acquired a handful of preferred walk-ons, and he thought enough of my potential and my character to include me in this group. The Hawkeyes wanted me to play football for them!

The University of Iowa would absolutely fulfill my goal of playing Big Ten football, and I was ecstatic. It felt great to be wanted! While my body was big for high school, it was tiny for college. Scholarship or not, I was extremely motivated to train hard and get bigger, stronger, and faster. No one would outwork me. I knew that I would prove myself, earn playing time, and eventually be rewarded with a scholarship. All I asked for was a chance, and now the Hawkeyes were offering one.

At the same time, the University of Iowa baseball program began to recruit me. On a visit to Iowa City in March of 1997, after accepting Coach Long's invitation to walk-on to the football team, my mom and I met with Iowa head baseball coach Duane Banks. Inside Coach Banks' office at Carver Hawkeye Arena, he shared his intention to offer a catching scholarship to one of four recruits. I was a finalist. He knew that I was on the football team but didn't care. We agreed that if I won the baseball scholarship, I could play both sports for one year and then have to make a decision. If baseball was paying my tuition and football wasn't, he explained, I would be expected to choose baseball. I verbally committed to his terms.

I left my Iowa City visit with a secure spot on the football team and in the running for a baseball scholarship. It was the perfect scenario and I could start to feel Hawkeye black and gold blood pump though my veins. All my college stress was gone, as I had already been academically accepted to the university. I knew two of the other catchers Coach Banks was recruiting; one eventually committed to Northwestern, the other to Vanderbilt. It came down to me and another player, so I liked my odds of being a scholarship catcher at the University of Iowa. Like my dad had said, all I had to do was keep doing what I had been doing.

Around the same time, I got a random call from Bill DeKraker, then the football recruiting coordinator at Indiana University. Coach DeKraker said he recently watched my VHS highlight tape, which had been sitting idly in his office since November. In a brilliant, extremely tempting recruiting move, he told me that Mike McGrath spoke highly of me and the coaches wanted to bring me to Bloomington for a visit. No scholarship was available, but the chance to walk-on and play Big Ten football with a South legend was appealing. I heavily considered making the trip. But, I had committed to Iowa, and Iowa had committed to me. I remained loyal and declined the visit. Besides, the only thing better than playing with Mike McGrath would have been to "thump" him on national TV.

A short while later, no scholarships had been offered to anyone. To stay fresh in their minds, my dad and I drove to Evanston to watch Iowa play Northwestern. A few weeks later, Coach Banks appeared at a South baseball game and saw me throw out a runner trying to steal by 20 feet. I felt confident that I was very close to earning an Iowa Baseball scholarship. One late May morning, a few weeks before high school graduation, I got a call from Coach Banks. I felt my heart pounding as I envisioned him officially offering me the catching scholarship. Why else would he be calling? *With just weeks left in my high school career, I was seconds away from accepting a baseball scholarship to the same school I had agreed to play college football!* It was an absolute dream scenario — all my hard work and sacrifice had paid off. I had just turned 18 years-old, and it was about to be the best moment of my life.

But, Coach Banks was not calling to offer me a scholarship. He was calling to tell me that he had retired, effective immediately, and no scholarships would be given. He assured me that if the new Iowa Baseball head coach was hired from within the program, our arrangement of playing both sports would be respected (albeit without the scholarship). The conversation was an honorable move on his part; he easily could have disappeared and never talked to me again. I didn't know it then, but Coach Banks' abrupt retirement altered the trajectory of my entire athletic career.

*   *   *   *

I prepared for Iowa Football and Baseball the best way I knew how. I represented the South in the 1997 North-South All Star Football Game. There were four guys in my huddle who would eventually be NFL draft picks — Antwaan Randle El (Thorton, Indiana, Pittsburgh Steelers), Ryan Diem (Glenbard North, Northern Illinois, Indianapolis Colts), Justin McCareins (Naperville North, Northern Illinois, Tennessee Titans), and Mark Anelli (Addison Trail, Wisconsin, San Fransisco 49ers) — and the game was loaded with Division I talent. I also played on a college baseball summer team; I was the only player not-yet-in-college. Rising senior Aaron Nieckula, an All-Big Ten catcher from the University of Illinois, was my teammate. Whenever he caught, I studied him. He had a rocket arm, tremendous work habits, quiet confidence, and instant respect from the pitching staff. Once, when he was playing right field in a game at Saint Xavier University, Aaron caught a ball at the wall and fired a laser to me at home plate to easily nail the runner trying to score. I barely had to move my glove — it was incredible. He was a great teammate and leader; the exact player I aspired to be. I was fortunate to have him as a mentor and to show me how All-Big Ten catchers looked and acted. After college, Nieckula was drafted by the Oakland A's, and played four years in their minor leagues before becoming a manager in Oakland's system. My optimism was high and I believed I could follow in his footsteps.

After success in the All-Star football game and holding my own against more experienced college baseball players, I was proud of my summer and felt as ready as anyone could possibly be. As an Iowa Football and Baseball walk-on, I realized I was at a monetary disadvantage compared with my scholarship teammates. Simply put, the University of Iowa was paying for them to play, and they were not paying for me — yet. Walk-ons have fewer opportunities, so I had to stand out in other ways. I had to think differently; I had to act differently. I didn't drink alcohol, smoke, or experiment with any drugs (recreational or performance enhancing). I didn't go to parties. I was 100 percent focused on being a great Iowa Hawkeye student-athlete. But, I still needed goals. Aside from getting bigger, stronger, and faster, I needed clarity. So, I created a timeline for goals to be achieved:

FOOTBALL
Year 1: Redshirt, compete on scout team; get bigger
Year 2: Earn special teams playing time; get bigger
Year 3: Weigh 230 pounds; challenge for starting fullback position

BASEBALL

Year 1: Challenge for starting catcher position as a true freshman

Year 2: Solidify myself as the top catcher in the Big Ten

Year 3: Get drafted into MLB

* * * *

As hard as I trained, I ate poorly and didn't sleep enough. My recovery was nonexistent: It was the definition of overtraining. Even 18 year-old bodies need a break from catching doubleheaders and heavy squats. I followed my Hawkeye-issued strength training program, but did not see the physical gains. In fact, I lost weight and felt like crap. As I glanced in the mirror at a body that I didn't recognize, I thought, "Where the hell is the rest of me?" In August, when I arrived on campus for a football-mandatory physical examination, the scale read 183 pounds — which seemed way too light. The previous night we went to a family dinner at The Iowa River Power Restaurant, and I could barely chew. Something was very wrong. Doctors found a severely enlarged spleen and swollen, golf ball-sized lymph nodes in my neck and armpits. I spent my first day of college at the University Hospital, diagnosed with mononucleosis. The doctors said if this had not been discovered, any impact could have ruptured my spleen, and I would have died on the practice field. The medical staff made it clear there would be no football for six months.

Thanks to mono, I was one of the smallest guys on the team, as well as in the running back room. We had kickers and punters who were bigger than I was! Knowing I could not physically participate, I had to create a strong first impression in another way. Sitting alone in my Slater Hall dorm room and feeling sorry for myself was not an option. So, against medical advice, I went to practice — as an observer. I watched film with the running backs in Coach Larry Holton's meetings. I was on the field for practice, dressed in Iowa Football shorts and a T-shirt. I paid attention to scout team protocol. I studied the playbook. I tried to do as many mental reps as possible, so when these six months were up, I was ready. Whose job was it to make sure I was adequately prepared? Obviously, it was mine.

Meanwhile, Iowa announced Scott Broghamer as the head baseball coach. He had been an assistant under Coach Banks, so I was relieved that our arrangement was still valid. Early in the fall, I showed up at baseball walk-on tryouts to introduce myself to Broghamer. I felt that my presence at a baseball practice on an early Sunday morning showed good initiative. It was also a smart idea to develop a relationship with Broghamer, whom I had never met and barely spoken with. I was a sick-with-mono football player yet still found the strength to appear at baseball practice. Certainly, this was a glimpse into my discipline and dedication. I was tempted to throw a couple of balls to second base, but was afraid my spleen might explode. Broghamer knew of me, told me to feel better, and to be in touch when football season ended.

After six weeks, my spleen and lymph nodes returned to their normal size. I was "healthy" and medically cleared to play football, so the choice to return to practice was mine. I was still a severely undersized Big Ten football player, much less a full-sized fullback. The linebackers and defensive ends I was responsible for blocking were in the 230-250 pound range, so I was giving up at least 50 pounds. We were nowhere near the same weight class. I should have taken more time to get stronger and increase my muscle mass. But, in the moment, I felt continuing to miss practice — after being given the medical green light — was the wrong decision. Instead, in an effort to gain weight, I would walk to the Old Capital Mall's Taco Bell and eat ten crunchy tacos before going to bed.

On my first day of practice, before being cleared for contact, the training staff continued to monitor my health. Clad in a helmet and shorts, I jogged around the perimeter of the main field while they flanked me in a golf cart. I was excited to finally be doing something physical, even if it wasn't a football-related activity. Head coach Hayden Fry, observing from the sideline, motioned for me to run toward him. Coach Fry was a god in Iowa City. He was the head coach for 19 years and took the Hawkeyes to 14 bowl games, completely changing the culture of Iowa Football. As I approached, he put his hands on my shoulders, and looked through my face mask and straight into my eyes. "You feeling better, son?" he asked me. "Yes, sir," I replied. With that, he nodded and tapped me on the back of the helmet, a nonverbal cue to continue my conditioning.

Holy shit, I thought, *Coach Fry just talked to me!* Obviously, I had seen him at practice and listened to him speak during team meetings, but this was our first personal interaction. The conversation blew me away for two reasons: (1) He actually knew who I was and that I was sick; (2) He was not just a football coach but also a human being, expressing genuine concern like I was one of his grandchildren. It was a small gesture on his part but something that I have always remembered.

*   *   *   *

Like everybody else, I had to earn my scout team reps. By definition, scout team offense is supposed to prepare the starting defense for the upcoming opponent. Most scout team freshmen are redshirted, and do not play on Saturday, so scout team life is the opposite of glamorous. Our job was to run the other team's plays and give the defense a real-time look at what they'll see on game day. Former Hawkeye linebacker Bobby Diaco, then a graduate assistant who eventually became the defensive coordinator for both the Universities of Notre Dame and Nebraska, would show the offensive huddle a meticulously diagrammed note card. The instructions for all eleven players were neatly written on the card. All we had to do was find the X or O that matched our position, follow the sketch that explained our job, and run the play. It was simple. As a coach's kid, I could easily understand what I had to do — which put me in the minority. Coach Diaco's lifespan is probably a little shorter based on how mad he would get when scout freshmen couldn't read his note cards and screwed up the play. When he wanted it to, his voice could explode throughout the football complex.

Obviously, my adult brain now realizes that my "mono body" was too small for Big Ten football, but in the moment, it would have been real hard to convince me back then. At South, I was known for big hits and pancake blocks. On the offensive scout team in Iowa City, it was much different. I was not a physically dominant player, so I had to find creative ways to keep my assignment from making the tackle. I tried to use clean footwork and body positioning to get in the way just long enough for Ladell Betts or Robbie Crockett to sneak through the line of scrimmage — lucky for me, they didn't need much of a hole. Sometimes it worked, sometimes it didn't.

One of the more memorable times that it didn't was during a goal line defense drill. We were practicing indoors, inside the Bubble; the scout team offense versus the No. 1 defense with the football on the goal line. I don't remember what Big Ten offense we were simulating, but I do remember that my job was to kick-out the defensive end and clear the "C" gap. On paper, Betts would be right behind me and stride into the end zone, untouched. Then, the freshman scout team would madly celebrate our touchdown against the starting defense.

Skip Miller — a 6'3" 250 pound defensive end — was my blocking responsibility. He was much bigger, much stronger, and much faster than I was. His assignment was to crash the "C" gap, which meant that we were both trying to get our bodies to the same space at the same time. Laws of physics explain that two objects cannot occupy the same place at the same time, so one of us needed to be removed from the equation. He got there first, and I angled myself to fight for his inside shoulder, to stop his momentum and drive him from the hole. That idea works in theory, but in reality, when a Mini Cooper hits an F-150, the F-150 usually wins. We collided helmet-to-helmet, and I was a mosquito on Skip Miller's windshield. It sounded and felt like a baseball bat hit me in the head, and as my body flew backward through the air, I saw the white canvas of the Bubble's ceiling before I hit the ground, laying flat on my back. Although we were wearing our turf shoes, Miller absolutely "de-cleated" me. It was a cartoonish highlight-worthy play for him, and an embarrassing look for me. Coach Diaco, standing behind the offense and a key witness to this violent assault, yelled, "JESUS CHRIST, KENT, DEFEND YOURSELF!" It was excellent advice.

The football gods were cruel that day. Someone on defense had underperformed so coordinator Bob Elliott gave the dreaded order to, "Line it up and run it again!" The second attempt, with the defense knowing exactly what the offense was going to do, led to a similar result. At least it did for me: I got crushed again. Two plays; two maulings. As I picked myself up off the ground, I was thankful to still be alive and move onto the next play. Somehow, someone on offense had screwed up (possibly me) and Coach Elliot was livid, which meant that we had to run the same play for *a third straight time*. Even with my bell rung on back-to-back plays,

I was clear-headed enough to know that my approach wasn't working. Miller was absolutely dominating me in this one-on-one match-up, so for play number three, I needed to try something different. Football is the ultimate team sport, and if one person fails to execute, all eleven players suffer. No one cared that I was at a physical disadvantage; if I'm in the huddle, then it is expected that I do my job. My teammates were counting on it. The third time, I allowed him to pinch and hit him on his outside shoulder, driving him into the pile of lineman. I didn't kick him out of the "C" gap — like the note card told me to — but he was no longer a factor in the play. Betts, who would be drafted by the Washington Redskins and play 9 years in the NFL, expertly read the block and scooted past my outside hip and into the end zone. Charles Darwin's theory of evolution was not about scout team, but his ideas proved to be battle-tested. Either we evolve or we continue to get our ass kicked by guys like Skip Miller.

* * * *

All the scholarship players were guaranteed to dress for home games. Walk-ons did not share the same privilege. Some walk-ons dressed; some didn't. My goal was to dress and get my name on the back of a jersey. Since I missed the first six weeks and the season was half over before I could even practice, I needed to make a quick impression. My willingness to always jump into the scout team huddle — at fullback, tight end, or wide receiver — was rewarded. In Week 11 against Minnesota, I was on the Dress List. As I wandered around the changing room inside Kinnick Stadium, trying to look like I'd been there before (when clearly I hadn't), I saw my locker directly next to fellow running back Tavian Banks. In 1997, Tavian reached 1,000 rushing yards in the fewest carries of anyone in NCAA history, and like teammate Tim Dwight, played himself into Heisman Trophy contention. He was a living Iowa legend and NFL-bound; I was a skinny walk-on and a nobody. He was one of the most talented players on our team and in the Big Ten; I was one of the least talented. Shouldn't his locker be next to somebody else; somebody more important?

Dressed as #37 with KENT on the back, I could barely hide my pregame excitement — and I wasn't even playing! Jogging onto the field at Kinnick, hand-in-hand with my teammates in The Swarm, was one of the greatest experiences of my football career. With the energy of 70,397 screaming Hawkeye fans heating the stadium, the cold late-November weather faded away. We beat Minnesota and kept the Floyd of Rosedale trophy in Iowa City (nothing shouts "Midwestern victory" louder than a trophy of a pig). Shortly after, Iowa accepted a New Year's Eve invitation to the Sun Bowl. The Hawkeyes were bowl-bound for El Paso, Texas!

Although we lost to a Pat Tillman-led Arizona State, the bowl experience was amazing. I traveled and dressed for the game, my first (and only) time wearing the white #37 jersey. My parents took a small vacation to come to the Sun Bowl. As a football lifer, it was Terry's first bowl game. I felt proud to have them in El Paso. But, now that football was over, it was time to shift my focus toward baseball. Back home for

Christmas break, I returned to South and started throwing, hitting, and catching, trying to cram in as much baseball work as possible. I wouldn't be in top baseball condition — I had not played since August — but no excuses, it was time to earn my spot.

*   *   *   *

The Iowa Baseball team traditionally, was bad. They had won one Big Ten title in my lifetime and typically finished at the bottom of the conference. Since 1990, they had never gotten closer than third place in the Big Ten. They needed help. When I got to practice in January of 1998, I was excited to be part of the class that could turn the program around. While I obviously was not in peak baseball condition, I remained optimistic. As Coach Banks had explained to me, the Iowa catchers were high in quantity but low in quality.

After two days of baseball practice, Broghamer pulled me aside and awkwardly told me that because I was a football player, I would not be on the baseball team. He told me to stick with football because he was going to keep players that were committed to baseball year-round. The conversation was awkward for two reasons: Broghamer's eyes looked everywhere but at me; and it was the exact opposite of what Coach Banks had told me. I was not prepared for this outcome and offered little response. The idea that I could be cut from the Iowa Baseball team — for being an Iowa Football player — never occurred to me. Before it even began, my Iowa Baseball career was over.

This was my first time feeling "not wanted," and it sucked. The reason I was cut had nothing to do with ability. If I played terribly, if I were completely overmatched and obviously did not belong playing Big Ten baseball, then sure, cut me. But, I had been recruited to play baseball at Iowa. Coach Banks and I both thought I was good enough. Being punished for my lack of commitment was a brand new experience for me. I had always played two sports, and split my time accordingly. I was plenty committed. Now, I was being penalized for it. As the head coach, Broghamer's decision was final. It was a tough life lesson.

With a baseball-free winter and spring, by default, I was fully committed to Iowa Football. I went through the brutal off-season conditioning program, which at the time was the hardest training I had ever done. I gained 20 pounds — putting me around 205 — and was the strongest and fastest version of myself, but still needed to gain about 20 more if I expected to be competitive. During spring practice, which was the first spring since kindergarten that I was not playing baseball, I had an epiphany. How was I going to make it to the big leagues as an Iowa Football player? Shouldn't I be playing college baseball? If Broghamer didn't want me on his team, then shouldn't I be somewhere else? At the highest collegiate levels, it became clear that I had to cut ties with football in order to elevate my baseball career.

The 1998 spring football game was my last time putting on an Iowa Hawkeyes uniform. I wore a white #44 jersey with no name on the back, and caught a 5-yard pass from Kyle

McCann on the last play of the game. It was also the last play of my football career. As a fun-sized fullback, I knew I could not physically compete. I wanted to stay in Iowa City, but with no baseball and a body that was too small for football, it was time to move on. A journey that began with amazing potential quickly ended due to the cold realities of high-level college sports. All that remained was an official release from the Iowa athletic department so I could pursue college baseball at a different university.

Photo by Nebraska Athletics

LINCOLN

"EVERYONE HAS A PLAN 'TILL THEY GET PUNCHED IN THE MOUTH."
– Mike Tyson

It was great to be a Hawkeye, so it stung to pull the Iowa Football helmet-sticker off the Escort and tell people I was transferring. In the days before social media, people actually had to have conversations about what was happening in their lives; there were no status updates. I got home from Iowa City in early May, and needed to find a new school by August. In the summer of 1998, the internet was in its infancy, so gathering information and shopping myself around was difficult. In hindsight, I should have picked a new school before leaving Iowa City. My only requirement was that school number two be like school number one, someplace sports were crucial to campus identity. Other than that, I had no idea where I was going.

I also needed to play baseball. It had been a full calendar year since I had been in baseball shape, so finding a summer team on which I could get instant playing time was essential. I was referred to the Wheaton White Sox, managed by Bill

Slight. Wheaton played in a Chicagoland wooden bat summer league, with local talent from various Division I, Division II, Division III, NAIA, and junior college players. The league was competitive, but not preeminent. Bill was an ex-military, old school, crew-cut wearing, tobacco-chewing, South-Side-type-of-guy. He was a total badass and a dugout general. There was a rumor that during the winter Bill continued his Red Man Chewing Tobacco habit, but with no baseball field to spit on, would swallow the tobacco juice! True or not, it impressed the hell out of his team. It was totally gross but gave a glimpse into the type of man he was, and the type of player he liked. You had to be drink-your-own-tobacco-juice tough. Bill was in his late 60s, and had retired from a successful career with Amoco BP. Now, summer baseball was his life. In his younger days, he had been a shortstop and quarterback at the University of North Dakota before playing a few years in the Pittsburgh Pirates organization. Aligning with Bill Slight was my smartest college baseball decision, as he was one of the best coaches I ever had.

*   *   *   *

During the previous summer, which I had spent studying Aaron Nieckula, we had a teammate who played for the University of Nebraska. Brian Zubor was a rising senior left-handed pitcher that I caught a couple of times. I did not know him well, and he probably would not remember me. Randomly, I heard him talking about how much he liked playing in Lincoln. Somehow, that stuck in my mind.

I knew nothing about Nebraska Baseball, but everyone knew Nebraska Football. During its dominant national championship years, I found inspiration watching Husker fullbacks like Corey Schlesinger and Joel Makovicka play a huge role in the run-it-down-your-throat Nebraska offense. Plus, their Husker Power strength and conditioning program was the best in the country (South had adopted a modified version). Although I was no longer a football player, Nebraska athletics was a huge brand with legions of fans. A year later, Zubor's words remained in my head.

After visiting two southern schools, Terry and I drove to Lincoln and met with head coach Dave Van Horn inside his office at Buck Beltzer Stadium. Coach Van Horn had taken over as Nebraska's head coach the previous spring, and was in the process of developing the roster to his liking. He did not recruit me, had never seen me play, and had no history with me. All he knew of me was from recent phone conversations with Coach Fox and Bill Slight. Yet, he talked about wanting athletes, not just baseball players. He said there were many new faces in the program, and it was an exciting time for Nebraska Baseball. Coach Van Horn told us that the best players would play, regardless of walk-on or scholarship status — which was beautiful music to our ears. *Do you really need a piece of paper to tell you you're the best?* Since I had been a college football player with good high school baseball credentials, I was the type of athlete he was looking for. I was hoping for a chance, and he was willing to give it to me. Coach Van Horn put me on the team as a walk-on and assigned me jersey #44. It was a perfect fit so I transferred to the University of Nebraska to play college baseball for the Cornhuskers. Go Big Red!

*   *   *   *

Although Nebraska and Iowa are similar states — both connected by Interstate 80 and the Missouri River — being in Nebraska was not like being in Iowa. Iowa City, only three hours west of Chicago, is heavily influenced by the large population of Chicagoland kids. Hell, the states even share a border. Conversely, Lincoln, eight hours west of Chicago and in the heart of the Great Plains, does not share an Illinois border and had zero Chicago influence. Zero. Bears games were not on local TV. Big Ten football was not on local TV. WGN was a *cable* channel. I did not have a car on campus and was grounded in Lincoln until Thanksgiving, which made me feel disconnected from home and alone on my journey. It helped that many of my new teammates were from Canada, Texas, Hawaii, and California. Even though we were not locals, we were all proud to be Huskers and recognized that "There is no place like Nebraska" is an accurate slogan. (Texan Will Bolt was one of those teammates; he is the current University of Nebraska head baseball coach.) Nebraskans are classy fans; they proudly support their Huskers, have closets full of red clothing, and provide a special environment in which to play college sports. It is guaranteed that the crowd inside any Husker stadium resembles an unmistakable sea of Nebraska red.

As the 1998 school year started, so began fall baseball. Fall baseball is equivalent to spring football. Coaches use it as a time for personnel evaluations, especially with new players, to see what talent they have for the upcoming spring season. For me the previous ten fall seasons had been for football, so it was the first time I had ever played fall baseball. Days were filled with weight training in the early morning, classes until midday, practice in the afternoon, and study hall at night. It was a grueling schedule — much more structured than my experience in Iowa City. My performance was average — some good days, and some bad days. I hit .297 but my talent was definitely behind. A year of Iowa Football left my timing off, and my arm strength was inconsistent. I was happy to have survived the first fall season in Lincoln — everything was new and difficult. Upperclassmen Brian Johnson and Justin Cowan were both better catchers, putting me third on the depth chart. I looked forward to the off-season so I could narrow the gap between us.

Lacey Degnan was our strength coach, and we loved him. A young guy, he was only a couple years older than our team and looked just like us. Lacey had come from the Miami Dolphins and would leave a year later to be the University of Montana's director of athletic performance. Husker Power was developed by the iconic Boyd Epley, the literal founder of the National Strength and Conditioning Association (NSCA). Boyd was the first full-time paid strength coach in college history, and had an all-sport emphasis on Olympic lifting. Lacey modified Husker Power to make it specific to baseball, and it was extremely effective. Guys like my roommate Ken

Harvey — who would be drafted by the Royals and represent Kansas City in the 2004 MLB All-Star Game — were in the best shape of their lives. Lacey made training fun. Sure, he busted our asses and pushed us hard with the usual mix of lifting, sprints, and agilities, but he would also think creatively. We would play ultimate frisbee and touch football, something we never did in Iowa City. We ran like maniacs, but because we were "playing" and not grinding, we trained harder. Having fun had a direct impact on our effort levels. Lacey's style and energy strongly influenced the way I train and interact with my clients today.

I loved the off-season commitment of college baseball. I didn't come to college to be a normal student and have the lifestyle that normal students have. Most college kids were trying to figure out where to get the most beer for their money on Thirsty Thursday, but that wasn't me. I came to Lincoln to work. Before school, we had hitting sessions with coach Mike Anderson. After class, I caught bullpens with pitching coach Rob Childress, then had team strength and conditioning with Lacey in the afternoon. The day concluded with study hall at night. With no study hall on Fridays, I had defensive drills with Jeremy Talbot, our volunteer catching coach. Coach Talbot, now an assistant at the University of Louisiana, was the first catching guru I worked with besides Terry and his southern accent was hilarious to me. Like Lacey, he was a young coach and would put the gear on to perform the drills with us. He could show us exactly how it was supposed to look, which enhanced his credibility. I appreciated his expertise and commitment to making us better — Coach Talbot treated me like a full-scholarship bonus baby, not like a walk-on. After practice, it was time to eat in the Hewit Center.

Now known as the Herman Student Life Complex, the Hewit Center was a student-athlete mecca. It was the epicenter of the Nebraska athletic universe. Its walls were filled with portraits of Nebraska Academic All-Americans as well as other Husker academic achievements. It housed academic support, study hall, the weight room, and the Performance Buffet. The Performance Buffet was a high-level training table available for all students, even non-athletes. In Iowa City, my experience with training table was that it was mostly for scholarship football players. In Lincoln, it was for everyone (somehow, the food always tasted better during football season). Their commitment to all facets of athletic excellence was impressive.

As a walk-on at my second school and on my second sport, I continued to hold myself accountable socially. I still didn't drink alcohol, smoke, or party all night. I wasn't against drinking, smoking, and partying. It just wasn't for me. I chose to focus on what I came to Nebraska for: baseball. There was no Plan B. I was afraid that if I got caught underage drinking, fighting, failing a drug test, or doing anything stupid, I would be off the team and my career would be over. The fear of embarrassment was a strong motivator, so I was willing to make social sacrifices. Since I had no safety net, the instant gratification reward was not worth the risk.

* * * *

The 1999 season was great for the Huskers. We were 42-18, Big XII Conference Tournament Champions for the first time in school history, and reached an NCAA Regional. While on the 25-man roster, essentially as the bullpen catcher, I earned a varsity letter but did not play much. My job was to catch batting practice everyday and work in the bullpen. In all my years as a catcher, I had never caught batting practice before. As I watched our opponents in pre-game, most teams did not have anyone catching BP. I wondered why I was the only one doing it. I quickly understood that lessons learned in high school did not apply to college. Early in the year, we hosted Chicago State University. In an epic offensive game, we set NCAA records for runs, RBIs, and margin of victory, winning 50-3 in 7 innings. Yes, 50-3! The game was so lopsided that it was featured on ESPN's SportsCenter and in *Baseball America*. We kicked their ass so badly that even I got to play. In the first at-bat of my college career, with a ridiculous lead and no pressure, I struck out. *Fuck me*, I said to myself as I walked back to the dugout, ears burning with humiliation. I had visualized a much better result for my college baseball debut, and was disappointed in myself. Fortunately, the baseball gods were generous that day, and I got a chance for redemption. In my second at-bat, I swung at the first pitch and cracked a home run over the centerfield fence. It bounced off the batter's eye, more than 400 feet away. My first college hit was a home run, and a bomb at that! Per baseball tradition, someone retrieved the ball for me. After the season, I gave it to my grandpa, where it sat on his desk for 20 years.

While chicks definitely dig the long ball, I have never been considered a "home run hitter" and the odds that I would continue smashing balls over the fence were slim. But, I thought it would earn me more playing time. At South, making the most of an opportunity led to more opportunity. In Iowa City, fighting for scout team reps was rewarded. Not in Lincoln. I got two more at-bats the rest of the year and played in six of our 60 games. Yes, I was the third best catcher on our team. I understood my role, worked hard, and kept my mouth shut. I felt I was making the best of the situation, and like a third-string quarterback, tried to ready myself with mental reps. In the dugout, Coach Childress —now the head coach at Texas A&M University — was in charge of pitch selection and would signal to Johnson or Cowan what pitch he wanted. I sat next to him and helped the pitchers with their pitching charts. I paid attention to Coach Childress' process, and tried to understand why he called specific pitches in specific situations. I enjoyed being an apprentice and learning the art of outsmarting hitters. As a result of my work ethic and team-first attitude, I felt I had earned some playing time when the situation warranted it. Plus, I was improving every day and getting back to being the player I was before college football interfered.

College baseball revolves around the weekend games, which in the Big XII was a Friday-Saturday-Sunday conference series. It was usually the best competition in the most hostile environments, and I definitely did not expect to play. But, there were times I thought I had earned an occasional at-bat. We swept Kansas, outscoring them by 26 runs over the weekend. Everyone played except me. We had a 16-inning game at Iowa State, that lasted almost five hours. Everyone played except me. Our mid-week, non-conference games were usually in the comfort of the Buck. There were times when Coach Childress told me I was going to play, even start, one of the non-conference games. I would call my dad and tell him that Coach Childress said I was going to play, but it never happened. I would get to the park, excited to see the starting lineup. My name was never on it. Not only was I not starting, it was also likely that I didn't even play in the game. As a coach's kid, I deeply cared about what the coaching staff thought of me, so I kept my mouth shut. Nobody likes a player who bitches about playing time. I seethed on the inside but was silent on the outside.

I spent the majority of my practice time with Coach Anderson, Coach Childress, and Coach Talbot, all of whom I liked. They were funny, high-energy coaches who connected with their players. My interaction with Coach Van Horn was limited, as he worked with the infielders along with handling his head coaching duties. Our relationship was one-sided. I respected Coach Van Horn and considered him a good coach because we won games — he had quickly turned Nebraska Baseball into a national powerhouse. But, the respect was not mutual. There was a moment on a road trip to College Station when I was in the wrong place at the wrong time. During a loss to Texas A&M, in a weekend where we were thoroughly outplayed, Coach Van Horn was ready to erupt. In between innings, I moved from my normal spot at the front of the dugout to the rear — where the Gatorade was stationed. I thought a change of scenery might help our baseball karma. With my fresh cup of Gatorade, I stood in front of two teammates who were screwing around and flicking sunflower seeds at each other. I had barely taken a sip when Coach Van Horn crossed the length of the dugout, got right in my personal space, and with plenty of screaming and swearing, specifically singled me out in front of the whole team. I'm sure that the Texas A&M fans, witnessing this outburst from their seats, thought I'd done something unforgivable, when in reality, I had done nothing. Coach Van Horn told me he was going to send me home immediately (the logistics of which were realistically impossible, but the threat seemed genuine). He publicly embarrassed me for a crime I had not committed.

Rather than get into an in-game shouting match with the head baseball coach at the University of Nebraska, I stood there, tight-lipped, and took it. If I had been guilty, then yes, I would have deserved an ass-chewing. Obviously, he was mad about how we were playing, but his decision to take it out on me was unprofessional and undeserved. I was not the type of person to be "fucking around on his bench" and felt he needed to know that. After a couple days had passed, I knocked on his office door and explained that I was innocent. I felt that standing up for myself — after the fact — was right and a respectful gesture. As a man, I thought he would hear me, apologize, explain that getting swept by A&M had him in a bad mood, and we'd shake hands and move on. But, that's not what happened. Coach Van Horn was straightforward that he felt no need to apologize and as far as he was concerned, I *was* guilty of fucking around on his bench. *Wait... what?* That conversation was a crystal clear sign from my head coach about his true feelings toward me. And I missed it.

*   *   *   *

Unlike the previous year, I was returning to the same school with the same teammates and the same familiarity. My girlfriend was on the Scarlet Dance Team, and pitcher Brandon Penas and I rented a sweet apartment on Superior Street — life was great! I had another solid summer playing for the Wheaton White Sox, and was extremely confident heading into the fall of 1999. Besides, we were the defending Big XII Tournament Champions and loaded with returning and incoming talent. With Brian Johnson drafted by the Royals, Justin Cowan and I were the only experienced catchers for the upcoming season. We had two new freshman scholarship catchers, so fall practice would be a crucial competition. Now with sophomore eligibility, my goal was to earn more playing time and to be a left-handed bat to complement the right-handed, incumbent Cowan. But, Cowan had sustained an elbow injury and would only be a designated hitter; he would not catch or play defense all fall. More opportunities were about to come my way, and I was ready to take advantage.

As a left-handed hitter, I loved watching fellow lefties Mark Grace of the Cubs and Robin Ventura of the White Sox. Like Grace, I was a gap-to-gap hitter and didn't strike out much. Like Ventura, I always hit with an open stance. Since Little

League, the open stance felt comfortable because I could "see the ball" better. None of my previous coaches cared as long as I could hit. After the first week of fall practice, competing against my very-talented teammates, I was hitting over .400 and playing some of my best baseball. But, one conversation by the batting cage changed everything. Casually, Coach Anderson (who would be promoted to Nebraska's head coach from 2003-2011) told me there was no way I could compete with my open stance, and I needed to fix it if I expected to contribute. This was surprising news. I had known Coach Anderson for a full year and spent countless hours in the batting cage with him, putting in the work to make myself a better hitter. During all our prior encounters, he never once mentioned my stance. Never. Now, when I was performing well in a pivotal battle for playing time, I was expected to stop a successful process and make fundamental changes. If I had been struggling and unable to deliver consistent contact, then making mechanical adjustments is justifiable. But, this seemed like the wrong moment to implement a new plan.

Hitting is about comfort and hitters have rituals that reinforce comfort. Good pitchers will do their best to make hitters feel uncomfortable. As a 20 year-old, losing my open stance made me extremely uncomfortable. Instead of thinking about hitting, I was thinking about what my feet were doing and where they were in the batter's box. Closing my stance felt like a drastic change and my timing and hitting mechanics were off. I struggled and was visibly awkward. But, I badly wanted to play in Lincoln, and as a coach's kid, wanted to be coachable and follow Coach Anderson's instructions. So, I disciplined myself to stay after practice for solo work off the tee, trying to regain that elusive comfort before fall practice ended.

Early in the fall, during monotonous "pitcher fielding practice," I was doing a good job fielding bunts, throwing to various bases, as well as directing the pitchers where to throw the ball once they had fielded their position — basic tasks required of a catcher. During the drill Coach Childress announced to our group that "Brian Kent's ready to win a starting job." My ears perked up and I swelled with pride. Oddly, soon thereafter, I found myself playing the outfield. It was totally bizarre, because I had not played outfield since Little League. I was a below average outfielder and even had to borrow someone's glove; I only had a catcher's glove. Plus, we had five guys who would eventually be drafted as outfielders. What the hell was I doing out there?

A couple of weeks later, after wondering about my time in the outfield, I asked new catching coach and former Husker Andy Sawyers — now the head coach at Southeast Missouri State — why I was not catching. Sensing my suspicions, Coach Sawyers told me that when the 2000 season started, Cowan and I would be our catchers. However, if Cowan's elbow was still hurt and he was unable to play defense, then the majority of the catching duties would be mine. According to Coach Sawyers, the coaching staff had contemplated bringing in a junior college catcher to fill Cowan's position, but decided against it because I was the better option.

Cowan was the unquestioned returning starter; a soon-to-be All-American and finalist for the Johnny Bench Award, given to the nation's top collegiate catcher. He was undeniably number one. But, if he were injured, then it was great to hear that I was the next man up. Besides, catcher is such a physically grueling position that every team needs two, capable catchers. I was pumped, thinking that I had played my way into the lineup. But, Coach Sawyers' comforting words were in direct opposition to what I would soon hear from Coach Van Horn; eerily similar to the contrasting opinions of baseball coaches Banks and Broghamer in Iowa City.

Overall, I played well in the fall. While I battled through a new batting stance, I still hit .333. When the fall season ended, all players had private meetings with the coaches to discuss team goals, individual goals, performance, expectations, and what to work on in the winter. I didn't understand why they had changed my batting stance or why I was playing the outfield, but I enjoyed these meetings because I liked getting personal feedback from the coaches. I had arrived in Lincoln at the perfect time, and as one of the country's premiere programs, we were set to be dominant for years. I was proud to be a Husker and loved what we were accomplishing together. I was certain they would reward my hard work and progress, as I had improved dramatically from Year One to Year Two. I felt I was a guy that went about his business "the right way" and had waited patiently for this moment; maybe they would offer me a partial scholarship.

Throughout my high school and even elementary career, I was taught to appreciate my coaches and teachers and understand my role in the process. When I had a bad game, it wasn't the coach's fault — it was my fault. When I failed high school geometry, it wasn't the teacher's fault — it was my fault. The adults preached accountability and encouraged the power of individual choice. I chose to follow their directions and never had a problem being coached or accepting my role. Sometimes, my role was to be the team captain, other times — like on South's freshman "B" basketball team — it was to be the last guy on the bench (my sisters enjoyed calling me "bench butt"). If I didn't like my role, then I worked harder or played better until it changed.

My dad coached me hard but fair. With football he specifically coached the running backs and outside linebackers; with baseball, the catchers — my exact positions (we spent a lot of on-field time together). He was the first to reward a good play or to correct a bad one. There was no family favoritism. I began to understand his coaching style and developed into my own harshest critic. No one was harder on me than I was. The desire to advance fueled me, and effort mattered. I grew up believing that playing as hard as we can, for as long as we can, was the only way to respect the game. In Lincoln, I was extremely self-aware and understanding of the effort required for improvement. When I arrived on campus, I was not yet ready for Big XII baseball. I studied Brian Johnson and Justin Cowan and saw them succeed behind the plate. It was clear that if I was going to play like them, then I needed to make some changes. I didn't like catching batting practice and watching from the dugout, so I applied my effort into progressing as a ballplayer and an athlete, to make sure I showed the coaches that I deserved more playing time. *Making the most of opportunities leads to more opportunities.* But, none of my experiences had prepared me for my one-on-one meeting with Coach Van Horn.

In life, no critique could hit me harder or stun me more than his words did on that late fall afternoon. Even now, all these years later, I can still vividly recreate the experience in my mind — down to the clothes I was wearing — and have vowed to never speak to anyone the way he spoke to me. It started innocently with Van Horn asking me for a self-evaluation, both individually and of the team. I confidently told him as a team, we had a chance to be great and should aim for the College World Series every year. I also thought that I had earned more playing time than last year and deserved to be the 1-2 catching combo with Cowan. I was excited for his response and what new roles awaited me.

"You're not as good as you think you are," was his sharp reply and the entire tone of our conversation instantly changed; it was now hostile. Coach Van Horn proceeded to break me down, and the CIA would have been proud of his psychological approach. He told me that I would not be on the 25-man roster or travel to away games. Starting? I wouldn't play at all, he said. He told me that I couldn't hit and couldn't throw, and "as a walk-on college football player trying to play baseball," expectations had always been low for me. My role, which was minimal in 1999, would be even less in 2000. I was never going to play. As the barrage continued, my posture — which started sitting tall and proud — slumped to my elbows resting on my knees, as if trying to evade his verbal assault. This quickly turned into a personal attack. Van Horn asked me if I had even been recruited to play college baseball; passive-aggressively suggesting that no school in the country thought I was good enough. His arrogance absolutely crushed me. Never in my life had anyone spoken to me in this manner; not my father, not my grandfather, not my football coaches. He was scolding me and I had done nothing wrong. Van Horn's words stabbed through my heart like a samurai sword, and it felt like we were back in that Texas A&M dugout. In a Hail Mary attempt to generate some offense, I reminded Van Horn of what he told my dad and me — in this very office — about the best player playing, regardless of scholarship or walk-on status. He laughed and said he wasn't bringing in scholarship catchers to sit on the bench.

My self-worth in question, I summoned the courage to provide examples of this contradictory feedback. What both Coach Childress and Coach Sawyers had recently said was completely opposite of what Coach Van Horn was now saying. Van Horn — continuing to address me like a peon — immediately pivoted, telling me that both coaches must have been using me specifically to motivate other players. He reiterated that the coaching staff and my teammates unanimously agreed that I had below average Division I ability and there was nothing I could do to improve it. Nothing. My work ethic, team commitment, and individual progress over the past three semesters was irrelevant. Van Horn concluded that I was not good enough to play for him and if I didn't like his evaluation, then I should leave Lincoln. Van Horn ended our discussion by saying that if he were me, he would leave. His final verbal dagger rattled me to my core.

I left the meeting sick and burning on the inside with tears streaming down my cheeks. It was the most anger I have ever felt in my life. Instantly, a dark pit of rage surfaced inside my soul. Self-control prevented me from reaching across the desk, grabbing Van Horn by the throat, and punching him in the mouth. I disagreed with his entire assessment. He made it seem like I was a shitty baseball player and a shitty human. I knew when I arrived in Lincoln that I was never one of "Van Horn's guys." But, I felt he was lucky to have me walk-on to his program. Van Horn did not recruit Chicago; the third biggest city in the country. Jeff Blaesing, a scholarship pitcher out of Chicagoland's Lockport High School, came to Lincoln via John Sanders, the previous head coach. Even if he hated me, wouldn't Van Horn want to use me as a pipeline to start luring Chicago talent? My dad was a high school baseball coach, for fuck's sake. After me, South had a stretch of about ten Division I baseball recruits, a handful of which should have interested Van Horn. Nothing about this situation made sense. Shortly after our meeting, new Rawlings catchers gear arrived — equivalent to Christmas Day. The other catchers tore open the boxes and eagerly modeled their new equipment. Yet, my locker remained empty; there was nothing for me. It was another example of being embarrassed in front of the team.

What was I supposed to do now? Again, I felt unwanted and even worse, personally disrespected. While Broghamer questioned my commitment, Van Horn questioned my ability. I disagreed with both of them. Two different coaches, with two different career-altering opinions. Van Horn was clear I would not play for him, and if I did not play in college, how was I supposed to play professionally? I had already uprooted my college life once, did I have the balls to do it again? To my 20 year-old brain, the options were: (1) sit the bench in Lincoln, (2) quit baseball and be a regular college student, or (3) go play somewhere else.

After deep reflection and multiple discussions with my parents, I chose option one. I loved Nebraska Baseball and my teammates. I could suck up my pride and use Nebraska Baseball like Nebraska Baseball would use me. I was willing to be so good in practice that it made Van Horn look foolish. I could be the bigger man and a team player. But, a subsequent follow-up meeting with the entire coaching staff made it clear they shared Van Horn's evaluation. They tore into me, three against one, denying previous positive statements and destroying my spirit. I reached a mental breaking point — a place I had not been before and have not been since — that obliterated my confidence. I enjoyed working with Coach Anderson and Coach Childress, because they were good coaches whom I believed saw my potential. But, Van Horn had decided — probably long ago — that I was not part of his present or future. I believe his voice overruled the other two. I wanted to stay, but these coaches lost my respect. I could not spend three minutes with them, much less three more years. Lincoln was a great place and an amazing experience until it wasn't, signaling the end of my Husker baseball career. It happened so quickly, I barely talked to my teammates about it. I wrote them all a letter and slipped it in their lockers for a final good-bye.

Demonstrating how big butts are essential for blocking home plate.
Photo by The Daily Kansan

OMAHA

"TO THINE OWN SELF BE TRUE."
– Polonius, via Hamlet

It was clear that my college athletic career was in a tailspin. Neither football nor baseball had worked out as I envisioned, and I needed redemption. I was physically healthy but mentally wounded. After some soul searching, I shook off Van Horn's assessment. I did not believe his opinion to be fact. While not everyone has Division I baseball talent, I felt I had the skills — and demonstrated them — to compete in the Big XII and anywhere else. I needed to find a new school; to prove Van Horn wrong and prove myself right. The NCAA has specific transfer eligibility rules, and I avoided a penalty the first time because my transfer was from football-to-baseball. This second time, with a baseball-to-baseball transfer, my punishment was to sit out a year.

To complicate my decision making, I had a girlfriend — who would eventually become my wife — back in Lincoln. Jacque Glynn was a scholarship athlete on the Scarlet Dance Team, part of the Husker's Spirit Squad. She is a classically trained jazz, tap, and ballet dancer. Jacque grew up in Omaha and was also an NCA All-American at Daniel J Gross Catholic High School. We randomly met at the Hewit Center one Friday night, when she and her dance teammates shared a dinner table with me and my baseball buddies. While I could not have predicted that we would get married, I knew our relationship was special and worth continuing.

Jacque's parents, Roger and Carolyn, had lived in Omaha all their lives. Roger loved sports, especially baseball. As a hard throwing left-handed pitcher, he was selected by the Cincinnati Reds in the 16th round of the 1977 MLB Draft, and spent a few years in their minor leagues back when the Big Red Machine dominated baseball. Unbeknownst to me, he was in the stands that day against Chicago State, watching my college debut. Roger was aware of my situation in Lincoln, and wanted to help me find a baseball home. He knew that my end goal was professional baseball so he suggested that I consider the University of Nebraska-Omaha, a Division II program run by his friend and new head coach, Bob Herold.

Coach Herold, also an Omaha native, had an impressive resume. He spent many years playing and coaching in the Kansas City Royals organization and had a strong background in professional baseball. In fact, his Royals had recently drafted my Husker teammates Ken Harvey, Brian Johnson, and Justin Cowan. It seemed to be a great fit athletically, academically, and personally. In addition, Coach Herold said he had contacts with some of the elite college baseball summer leagues, and could help send me to one. I loved playing for the Wheaton White Sox, but wanted to test myself against higher profile competition. Many of my Lincoln teammates were sent to these elite summer leagues, and I wanted to go, too. I trusted that Coach Herold could help me. Knowing I would sit out the 2000 season, I transferred to Omaha — school number three. I was willing to sacrifice another college season to further my pro career. Hell, I barely had anything to show for a college career at this point, so I was putting all my chips on the table for the 2001 season. I was betting on myself to do what I believed I could do: Play well and get drafted by an MLB team. As a transfer-ineligible player, I was given jersey #34 for the Mavericks.

*   *   *   *

After watching the 2000 season from the stands, I was obsessed with playing summer ball for the Wheaton White Sox. Bill Slight's other catcher quit the team, so I caught every game, including doubleheaders. It was the first time since high school that I was the primary catcher, and it was exactly what I needed to remind myself that I could be a future pro. I batted third in the lineup and hit .335. My defense was great — I did not commit an error or allow a passed ball, and threw out 20 of 34 baserunners. At the conclusion of the season, I was voted the team MVP. That summer, Bill and I had many talks about life and baseball. He was my biggest supporter. He disagreed with Broghamer and Van Horn and thought I was as good as any catcher on TV. He understood my mentality, my drive, and allowed me to be comfortable. Bill was a great man and told me to trust myself. He had once coached Dan Wilson and told me I was a better player. Wilson, the epitome of a defensive catcher, played 14-years in the big leagues and ended his career with a .995 fielding percentage, the highest in American League history. Bill's confidence in me reinforced my belief that I could be a major league catcher. I considered myself to be a student of the game and tried to watch as many MLB games as basic cable allowed. Joe Girardi of the Cubs, Mike Matheny of the Cardinals, Charles Johnson of the Marlins, Jason LaRue of the Reds, Jason Varitek of the Red Sox, Jorge Posada of the Yankees, Jason Kendall of the Pirates, and Pudge Rodriguez of the Rangers were some of my favorite catchers. I studied them. They all had different skill sets that I applied to my own game. The more I watched, the more I was convinced I could do what they did.

In addition, I tried to blaze my own path by attending every Chicagoland MLB tryout camp. While no one leaves a tryout camp with a signed contract, a strong performance can increase scout interest. I had transferred twice and barely played any college baseball, so I needed all the hype I could get. MLB tryout camps are comparable to the NFL Combine, at which players perform a small sample size of baseball-specific drills. For catchers, that meant "pop-times." Pop-time is defined as the time it takes for the ball to "pop" the catchers glove — including a quick transfer and throw — until it "pops" the middle infielder's glove down at second base. The drill predicts how likely a catcher is to throw out a potential base-stealer, and any throw under 2.0 seconds is considered a professional time. I had been under 2.0 since I was a junior at South. I went to tryout camps for the Florida Marlins, Chicago Cubs, and Montreal Expos. Most of my throws were in the high 1.8s to low 1.9s, negating Van Horn's theory that I couldn't throw. The scouts said they would be ready to watch me play in the spring.

Returning to Omaha for my first fall season as a Maverick, Coach Herold rewarded me with a partial scholarship. In my seventh college semester, I was a scholarship student-athlete! Sure, it was Division II, but finally, everything was coming together. It seemed like transferring to Omaha was the right decision. But, my body was tired. All those summer games had taken their toll, and while I still did my strength and conditioning, I needed a baseball break. No one in Omaha knew about my great summer and tryout camp performances, so I felt obligated to push myself through fatigue. I had to prove to my new teammates and coaches what kind of a player I was, which ended up being a critical mistake.

* * * *

It was apparent that Omaha was a Division II school. I was extremely spoiled in Iowa City and Lincoln, with Division I facilities, Division I attention-to-detail, and Division I budgets. The Hawkeyes were sponsored by Reebok, and all our gear was school-issued. The Huskers were sponsored by Adidas, and we dressed like a team at all times. The Mavericks were clearly a step down from what I was used to. They had no campus baseball stadium; but instead shared a city park with many Omaha high school teams. South's baseball field — which doubled as a football practice field and was not great — was better than Omaha's home field. At fall practices, some guys wore their high school hats. Some showed up wearing sweat pants. Some guys wore Nike, some guys wore Adidas. Compared to where I had been, it was a drastic change. It seemed like the commitment level was lower, and it felt more like high school baseball than college baseball. Socially, it was also different. In Lincoln, guys hung out at each other's dorm rooms or apartments all the time. But, Omaha was a commuter campus, and the majority of players were local and lived with their parents. There was little team cohesion off the field. It was an odd dynamic, further fueled by Coach Herold and assistant coach Chris Gadsen instituting a team no-swearing policy. Swearing went against their Christian values. I'm all for discipline, but asking 18 to 22 year-olds not to swear was ridiculous. This was a baseball team, not a church group. But, I was from out of town and my feelings were in the minority.

However, I could train myself to look past all the program oddities and focus on baseball. The 2001 season was the most important year of my life. I would finally get the chance to prove myself — and I was ready to shine. My plan was simple: Duplicate my summer success. Whatever happened after that was beyond my control, but I was ready to get drafted and be done with college. Our first games were against Division I Creighton University. Creighton is also located in Omaha, but due to weather conditions, we played at Wichita State University — in Wichita, Kansas (the absurdity of driving across state lines to play an opponent located 10 minutes from campus was not lost on me). Catching game two of the doubleheader, in my first college game for the Mavericks, I threw out a couple of runners and scored a run. On the bus ride back to Omaha, my right — throwing — shoulder started to ache.

At first, I ignored it. Every baseball player deals with a sore elbow or shoulder; it's the nature of a sport that demands the stressful, unnatural arm motion required to throw a ball. I tried to will away the discomfort. There was never a good time to get hurt, but this was the worst time. As the season progressed, the pain increased and my performance suffered. The ability to cock my arm back and throw was compromised. I lost trust in my ability, and ultimately in myself. I struggled offensively and had a horrible junior year, hitting .105 (in only 38 at-bats) before shutting myself down due to the pain. The training staff worked on my shoulder, but concluded that nothing was seriously wrong. All I knew was I had endured the worst season of my life and that my arm hurt. My statistics were embarrassing. As a catcher who loved throwing people out and picking runners off bases, I could barely throw the ball back to the pitcher. This was not a mental problem, as was suggested to me. Something was physically wrong. My baseball future was unclear, but certainly no pro team would draft an injured Division II player — especially with a .105 batting average.

I came home for the summer, played for Bill, and worked as a laborer for Passarelli Builders and Design. The opportunity to compete in an elite summer league never presented itself; another college baseball disappointment. My arm was still in pain and not improving, but I was trying to gut it out. Bill knew

I was hurt and reluctantly put me in the lineup. Although my workload was reduced, I managed to hit .320 and threw out 7 of 12 baserunners. I wondered why, statistically, I played well at home but not in Omaha. My shoulder hurt in both locations but the results were significantly better with the Wheaton White Sox. The situation had me flummoxed.

One afternoon, I received a letter in the mail from the University of Nebraska-Omaha athletic department. It read:

Your baseball scholarship for the 2001-2002 school year is: $0.00

A subsequent call to Coach Herold led to a heated discussion about my 2001 performance not being scholarship-worthy. I explained that I played poorly because I was injured, not because I sucked. He countered that as a non-scholarship athlete, I was no longer affiliated with the baseball program and expected to clean out my locker. If I wanted to continue playing in Omaha I had to tryout and walk-on, with no guarantee that I would make the team. My Omaha reality included a hurt shoulder, a fading career, and now, a lost scholarship. I needed to know what was wrong with my arm.

Dr. Marc Asselmeier was an orthopedic surgeon and a shoulder expert. The license plate of his car read "SHLDRS," which I hoped was a sign that he was good at his job. While the MRI showed no visible tears, my painful reactions to his manual testing suggested otherwise. I could not lift my arm over my head without pain. With continuous discomfort for six months, a severe decrease in athletic performance, and a baseball career hanging by the tiniest of hope, it was time to fix the problem. Dr. Asselmeier suggested arthroscopic surgery, and told me that if I agreed to the procedure, there was a chance I would never play again. With nothing else to lose, I had to take the gamble. Surgery was set for Tuesday, September 11, 2001.

There are no words to describe how terrible 9/11 was for the United States and the world. After arriving at the hospital, my surgery was massively delayed. For hours, my mom and I sat in my pre-op room watching the chaos on TV. Every channel reported the same news, and there was talk that Chicago might be the next terrorist target. The entire hospital was extremely stressed and on high alert. When Dr. Asselmeier informed us it was go-time, the fate of my baseball career rested in his surgical hands on the scariest day in recent American history.

Upon regaining consciousness, Dr. Asselmeier relayed that the "scope" was successful, and that he drilled three small holes in my shoulder. The supraspinatus muscle of my rotator cuff was torn — which had not shown up on the MRI. Plus, there was an impingement and a loose ligament — typical shoulder problems from years of throwing a baseball. Dr. Asselmeier put me in an immobilizer-sling that rendered my right arm useless, and said he would fax my rehab instructions to the athletic trainers in Omaha. The injury perfectly explained the pain I was having; it was likely caused from overuse, not from one specific trauma. I was relieved to know there really was a physical problem. He reiterated that the road to recovery would be long and tedious.

*   *   *   *

There was a major point of contention that delayed my physical therapy. I had made doctor's appointments and scheduled an out-of-state surgery without first consulting the Omaha medical staff. Since I was no longer a scholarship-athlete, and my surgery was not performed by an Omaha-appointed surgeon, the Omaha training staff felt no obligation to help with my rehab. I argued that since I was injured playing Omaha baseball, and sought documented treatment during the Omaha baseball season, I deserved their care. They agreed to help me in "good faith," but refused to follow Dr. Asselmeier's aggressive rehab plan. The disconnect between my surgeon and the Omaha training staff put me weeks behind schedule. It was yet another setback on a long road to recovery, contributing to the anger and frustration that was festering inside me.

I had no intentions of playing the 2002 season, which would have been my senior year. Even if my arm were healthy, which it wasn't, I was done with college baseball. My time in Omaha was miserable, and I was mad at myself for not achieving any goals. Meanwhile, the Huskers had gone to the College World Series back-to-back in 2001 and 2002 — in Omaha's famed Rosenblatt Stadium. I watched some of my best friends playing on ESPN, and I was jealous. They were on top of the college baseball world, while I was sitting on my ass with my arm in a sling. Many of my former teammates were drafted, and Ken Harvey, Dan Johnson, Shane Komine, Adam Shabala, Adam Stern, and Jamal Strong would all make it to the big leagues. They deserved it, and I was happy for them. But, privately, I raged. I wanted what they had, but I was so far from where they were. They had great college careers and professional contracts. I had neither. Had Instagram existed in the early 2000s, I could picture myself falling victim to depression. To scroll through my phone and watch former teammates posting pictures and videos of their glorious victories would have absolutely crushed me. Because it was my decision to leave Lincoln (the coaches may have pushed me to the edge, but it was me who jumped), I would have scrutinized every past, present, and future decision. I would have forever questioned myself and there is a strong chance "paralysis by analysis" would have dragged my life into a pit of quicksand.

While I was glad to earn my degree, I was even happier to be done with college. Here was my reality: Five years, three schools, two sports, one illness, and one surgery. As a Hawkeye football player, I was sick, redshirted, and did not play; as a Husker baseball player, I barely played; and as a Maverick I got hurt and played like shit. I had a redshirt year, a transfer sit-out year, and a surgery rehab year — three years with no playing time. It was nothing like the career I had envisioned for myself. This was not the path to the big leagues.

One of the hardest parts of post-surgery rehabilitation was the mental battle. Most major surgeries take a full calendar year to heal physically, but healing mentally takes even longer. Seeing the cumulative atrophy in my right arm was a daily reminder of how far I needed to go. My muscles had deteriorated to the point that when I would work out with Jacque, she could easily lift heavier weights than me. My patience was constantly tested and I questioned if I would ever play again. The majority of my rehab exercises were the same exercises I had done for years. As a sport, baseball knows arm injuries are an epidemic, so shoulder maintenance programs are implemented in high school. We did them at South. If the exercises selected to heal me were the same exercises that were supposed to protect me, how did I get hurt, and why did it happen now? I had done everything right to shield my arm from injury, yet it still broke down. There were plenty of questions that had no answers.

Not only did my arm need to heal and get back to basic functioning, I also needed to relearn how to throw a baseball. Repeating the very act that injured my shoulder was the most pivotal part of the rehab. Before surgery, throwing a baseball had been involuntary, like scratching an itch. After surgery, with an arm that was disconnected from my brain, the motion felt foreign. I had to create brand new thoughts about: Arm angle, elbow height, wrist position, and follow through. Thinking about performing a simple task, before performing a simple task, is usually a terrible combination for baseball players. When I was cleared to start throwing, it looked more like "fetch" than catch as my accuracy was horseshit. The bitterness of a failed college career, an arm that betrayed me, and the inability to perform basic movements left me in a bad mental state. I was ready to get the hell out of Omaha.

* * * *

The Kansas City Royals Triple-A team was in Omaha, and the 2002 Omaha Royals needed a bullpen catcher. As a recent college grad with a bad arm and no job, I accepted. The O-Royals were managed by the legendary Bucky Dent (yes, *the Bucky Fuckin' Dent*) and treated me as well as their players. In addition to catching all the pre-game bullpens, I got to take batting practice (professional catchers don't catch batting practice) before each game, and work in the bullpen during the game. I caught all their nasty relievers, played catch to rebuild my arm strength, and enjoyed the day-to-day of minor league life. Baseball was fun again. I was not healthy enough to play, but I worked on getting better each day. It was the perfect use of my time. Everyone on that team was trying for daily improvement to move up the ladder, and I was the same. I was just on a much, much, much lower ladder.

In the bullpen, I wore full catchers gear and pretended it was my game day. I worked on my receiving and blocked everything in the dirt. The O-Royals sent many pitchers to the big leagues that summer including Shawn Sedlacek, Brad Voyles, Chris George, Ryan Bukvich, and Mike MacDougal. So, I caught Kansas City's best prospects. Handling the Triple-A pitchers, albeit only in the bullpen, started to rebuild my confidence. If I could catch their nasty sinkers, cutters, and split-fingered fastballs, I could catch anything. I just needed to get healthy.

Applying judo's principles of maximum efficiency and minimum effort helped boost my career. Photo by Will Edwards

FIGHT

"THE FIRST AND GREATEST VICTORY IS TO CONQUER YOURSELF."

– Plato

Here were the facts: I was 23 years-old, living at my parents house, no tangible baseball future, a college batting average of .119, and an arm that had betrayed me. Also, there was a race against time. If I had not been drafted in high school or college, then what more could I show that I hadn't already shown? Plus, there was a younger crop of talent right behind me. Like a used car lot, out with the old and in with the new! Even if a scout tried to find me, it took more effort to follow my career — which zig-zagged across Interstate 80 — than it was worth. The reality was that if I were serious about my slim chance at professional baseball, I needed to heal my mind as well as my body. I had been mentally defeated and physically broken. Before I could help a baseball team, I had to help myself first. I needed to transform my mind and my body into a weapon; I needed to regain confidence in myself as an individual and find my fighting spirit. While I proved I could handle a *beating*, I could not accept being *beat*.

I prided myself on being a different type of athlete. Especially as a walk-on, and now as an undrafted free agent, I needed something to be special about me. There is just too much competition — for so few roster spots — to be complacent. It was not enough to *just be a football player*, or to *just be a baseball player*. If my resume was the same as everyone else's, then I held no advantage. What did I have or what could I offer, that everyone else didn't or couldn't? What could I do to separate myself? How could I show that I was better prepared, or that I wanted it more? For a long time, football and baseball complemented each other. If I caught a pass on the football field, coaches said, *he's also a catcher*. If I won a collision at home plate, scouts said, *he's also a fullback*. But, I hadn't played football in four years — it was part of my history but not part of my present or future. I needed a new way to be different.

*   *   *   *

As a child, I loved Batman and the Teenage Mutant Ninja Turtles. I wanted to be a ninja superhero. When I was 7 years-old, we moved into our home on the south side of Downers Grove. There was no furniture in the front room, so it became my private dojo to practice ninja-superhero techniques. Terry and Juli started me in karate, but with Little League, Pee Wee football, and YMCA basketball, karate became less of a priority. I never lost interest, just became too busy. As I got older, and my commitment to South increased, there was no time for anything extra. But now that I was home from college without a baseball job or a real job, I had plenty of availability.

Lions Martial Arts, located on 75th Street in Woodridge, was a Korean martial arts school specializing in taekwondo, hapkido, judo, and kickboxing. It was 10 minutes from my parents house. While I was nervous about injuring myself, I scraped together what little money I had and signed up. After a couple of classes, it became apparent that it was a great decision. I set a goal to earn a black belt faster than I had earned my college degree.

Masters Chun Kim and Chang Yoon were studs. They both held black belts in multiple martial arts and were great teachers. They ran a disciplined school, which was an instant attraction. Class started with a seated meditation, forcing me to be alone with my thoughts. I hated it. But, the point of the meditation was to sit quietly and clear our minds of distractions. By focusing on what we were about to do, we could stay mentally present and leave our stress outside the dojang. We were supposed to breathe through our bellies, and be aware of how our breath affected our concentration. As someone who had become easily distracted, it was difficult for me to "do nothing." Sitting still was torture, so I would open one of my eyes, look around at the students who were following directions, and find my mind constantly wandering. Then I would get mad. Why the hell was it so hard to focus? How were the easiest instructions proving to be massively difficult? If something so simple was hard for me, then clearly I needed to work on it.

But, was this indicative of a larger problem? Most athletes play better when they are relaxed. My athletic life was still on a downward trajectory, and I was really fucking stressed. If I struggled to focus and breathe properly in a controlled setting, how could I expect myself to perform well in a high-stakes competitive environment? My mind had been infected with a terrible disease: doubt. When Dr. Asselmeier said there was a chance I might never play baseball again, doubt latched onto me like a parasite, leeching away my confidence. Anytime I made a bad throw, I cussed my shoulder and doubted myself. During the rehab summer with the O-Royals, I played catch with the pitchers to build back my arm strength. If I overthrew my partner, or bounced one at his feet, I would immediately doubt if my arm would ever return to its pre-surgery form. Doubt destroyed my confidence. Dr. Asselmeier should have said that if I followed his protocol exactly, trusted the process and allowed time for my shoulder to properly heal, I would come back stronger than before. Confident minds are needed to perform at the highest level, and there is no place for doubt inside a confident mind.

The physicality of taekwondo came naturally. As an art that specializes in kicking and punching, my athleticism and flexibility allowed me to quickly pick up the proper striking mechanics. I loved exploding through targets with different parts of my body and having the hand-eye and foot-eye coordination to connect with force. The science behind the art made perfect sense: Kicking with the whole body is more powerful and efficient than kicking with just a leg; punching with the whole body is more powerful and efficient than punching with just an arm. My mind started to pair martial art philosophy with athletic performance. Was I using my full-body on the field? Was I producing as much power as my frame should have allowed? Was I properly channeling my energy? Was I being efficient with my movements?

*   *   *   *

All rookie martial artists start out as white belts. It might be intimidating to step on the mat in a room full of people who are more experienced and better fighters, but part of the martial art code is that the higher rankings are expected to help the lower rankings. The five tenants of taekwondo were posted on the wall: Courtesy, Integrity, Perseverance, Indomitable Spirit, and Self-Control. They served as a written reminder that we weren't just there to beat the shit out of each other — there was a purpose to how we were training. Lions provided a home and an atmosphere to work on myself as an individual, to put the focus specifically on Team Brian. I appreciated the attention and I was learning physical movements with an emphasis on mental clarity — as it turned out, it was the perfect cure for doubt.

Truthfully, I was an angry person. College sports had severely punished me, and I had a negative mindset. Throughout the countless hours of Lions technique, drilling, and sparring, fatigue was inevitable. As in sports, the question was how much discomfort could I handle before succumbing? When I would feel myself getting tired, all I had to do was tap into one of those forever-remembered conversations with Broghamer, Van Horn, or Herold. As soon as I began to visualize and mentally re-create those experiences, the anger and rage energized me. Every time I hit the heavy bag, I imagined I was hitting them.

I was used to fighting. I fought for playing time, a roster spot, a scholarship offer, and against my coaches. But, Lions was a different kind of fight. Instead of fighting *against* others, I was fighting *for* me. My mental and physical well-being was now the priority, and the foundation for inner confidence was built. My pain threshold, plus my ability to handle stress and perform well, increased each time I was on the mat. I could put my mind into a place that effectively fought my demons and began to therapeutically heal my soul. I decided that I defined me; not my college coaches.

*　*　*　*

The curriculum at Lions was like an individualized education plan, and effort was rewarded. Because I had plenty of free time, I got to class three nights a week. The more I practiced, the more I improved. The more I improved, the more stripes I earned for my belt. The more stripes I earned for my belt, the quicker I was up for a belt promotion. The quicker I was up for a belt promotion, the closer I got to earning a black belt. The closer I got to earning a black belt, the closer I was to reaching my goal. I did not achieve many of my college goals, so I was craving success somewhere in my life. The best part was that success was directly related to my effort and commitment. I could control the process, which led to the desired outcome. While Lions provided the structure and encouragement, it was my job to provide the work. The math was simple: Effort + Consistency = Reward.

On a behavioral level, martial arts — like sports — revealed true character. Lions sparring sessions were kickboxing-based, so there was a good chance I would be cracked by someone's foot or fist. Getting punched and kicked hurts, but as a catcher and a fullback, I enjoyed physical contact. I had been verbally punched and kicked during the past five years, so instead of being caught square, I was ready to deflect these blows and launch an attack. Martial arts are not always about fighting, they also offer a platform for self-reflection. I realized that I had been on defense for far too long, as I did not have the DNA to verbally engage with my coaches. Now, a quick redirection of energy was an efficient method to take control of the fight. When backed into a corner, we have two choices: Cover up and take the beating, or find a way to fight out of it. I had been beaten down, but now was ready to fight back. Fighting out of a corner is extremely hard, but so is batting with an 0-2 count, or blocking a blitzing linebacker. The mentality to battle is the same. If we're down, let's start chipping away until we're up. If we're out, let's go out swinging.

While I earned my black belt in four years, my attendance dropped dramatically before my final exam. After I moved out of my parents house and into my first Chicago apartment, I could only get to Lions on Saturdays. I had to discipline myself to put in hours of solo practice to memorize and review the various katas, punching and kicking combos, and self-defense techniques required to pass the test. I could have been satisfied and made excuses that Lions was no longer convenient, but I had committed to them and Master Kim and Master Yoon had committed to me. They were my new coaches, and there was no way in hell I would disappoint them. I took the early Metra train every Saturday morning to make that class. I often had to sprint down the terminal, as train doors were closing, to guarantee my showing up. It was important for me to honor my commitment.

*   *   *   *

Lions also had a Wednesday night judo class. Judo, a Japanese grappling martial art, was nothing like taekwondo. We subbed our normal, lightweight gi for the heavier, thicker, judogi — a new addition to my ninja wardrobe. Terry coached wrestling for many years, and used to wrestle me all over the house. There was something extremely discouraging about being pinned to the ground by a larger man, while he rubbed his scratchy mustache on me. I didn't like it. As a high schooler, I thought the skimpy, spandex, wrestling singlet was a ridiculous looking uniform, so I played basketball. But, the judogi looked nothing like a singlet and I was intrigued. The art of unbalancing someone by pushing and pulling was interesting. Facing a resisting opponent, who was equally trying to unbalance me, piqued my curiosity. The proper execution of a judo throw was beautiful, effortless, and powerful. I had to branch out and learn more.

Tohkon Judo Academy was located in Chicago's Uptown neighborhood — eight blocks north of Wrigley Field. Sensei Douglas Tono — a 7th degree black belt — was the head instructor, but he carried a deep roster of black belt coaches that included former Olympians, US National Champions, European National Champions, Sambo World Champions, and Brazilian jiu-jitsu champions. They were considered a "fight dojo" and competed globally. I was not looking to be a competitor, but Tohkon was full of inspiring trophies and gold medals. It was easy to realize I was surrounded by great people, all with high levels of success on and off the mat.

While taekwondo had their five tenants, judo had a creed of "mutual benefit and welfare," and "maximum efficiency with minimal effort." I understood mutual benefit and welfare: When two partners practice together, they each benefit from working with the other; each person makes their partner better. *Maximum efficiency* I also understood, but *minimal effort* was hard to grasp. As an athlete, *minimal effort* is a one-way ticket to the bench, possibly off the team. I struggled with the interpretation, but Sensei Tono phrased it like this: Only using as much effort as the job requires; anything else is wasted energy. For years, I felt like I had been figuratively killing ants with a sledgehammer. If I could use my energy better, I could play better. This was a whole new way of thinking and a contrast to my previous mindset.

While taekwondo came easily, judo was hard. My brain understood what I was supposed to be doing, but my body had a difficult time actually doing it. There was a big difference between muscling someone and using technique. Great technique took skill and leverage, while muscling was for amateurs. It was humbling to struggle with something physical, so I had to put in extra work to do it right. Compared with team sports, judo also had completely different goals. In baseball, the pitcher tries to get the hitter out; the hitter tries to get a hit — they have opposing goals. In football, the offense tries to score; the defense tries to stop them — they have opposing goals. In judo, the goal is the same for both fighters: Throw the other guy to the ground and submit him. Whoever could do it better or quicker usually won. If I got beat in practice — which happened often — then it was because my partner was better than me. There was no one to blame and no excuses to be made, it was all on me. Stepping onto the mats reinforced personal accountability — more inner strength for Team Brian. It took 11 years of consistent training, but eventually I earned my black belt from Tohkon. Receiving my Shodan from Sensei Tono was one of the most satisfying moments of my athletic career.

Initially, the ne waza aspect of judo was humbling. Being able to effectively move my body from a myriad of ground positions was a new experience, and I thrashed around like a beached whale. My movements were sloppy, inefficient and full of energy leaks. I outweigh Sensei Tono by 50 pounds but he could easily dominate me on the mat. He would nullify my size advantage by driving his full bodyweight into one part of my chest, and I would be pinned to the ground. If my life depended on it, I could not escape and it blew my mind that little guys could hold me down. I had to learn how to use my body more efficiently.

Professor Tony Williams was a former University of Wisconsin running back, a two-time Rose Bowl champion, a black belt in Carlson Gracie Brazilian jiu-jitsu, and an excellent personal trainer. Prior to becoming a trainer, he was a strength coach at the University of Iowa and a scout for the Chicago Bears. Pound-for-pound, Professor Williams is one of the strongest human beings I have ever seen. At 5'11" and 190 pounds, he has zero percent body fat. His workouts are so impressive that I will stop to watch whatever he's doing. His muscles seem to have developed their own muscles, because the dude is ripped. As a football player and athlete, he had a great mind for coaching and teaching. I enlisted his expertise to help me better understand both arts, which meant more countless hours grappling, drilling, and sparring. Professor Williams was 100 percent better than me, so the majority of my initial training revolved around surviving from bad positions. Early on, he would fiendishly test me by giving just a little bit of room to maneuver — and a sliver of hope that I could escape — only to slam the door and make me fight harder and longer. It required my brain to completely focus on the immediate situation. If my mind drifted, even for one second, there was an outstanding chance I was strangled or submitted. Rolling with Professor Williams required my full attention. It was mentally and physically grueling, and completely tested how long I could maintain my concentration.

As a catcher, maintaining concentration is extremely important. The more I could focus amidst chaos, the more I could help my team. Catchers have to be mentally locked-in for each pitch; they are not allowed to be preoccupied with extraneous thought. If Professor Williams felt like my mind was elsewhere, he would easily apply physical pressure to remind me to focus on our current situation. Often, I had to ask myself, *am I in pain or just uncomfortable?* If the answer was pain, it was time to tap out. If I was just uncomfortable, then hell, we trained to be comfortable being uncomfortable. While exhausted, overmatched, and completely uncomfortable, I had a choice: quit or grit. I chose grit.

*　*　*　*

My experiences at Lions Martial Arts with Masters Kim and Yoon, Tohkon Judo Academy with Sensei Tono, as well as Brazilian jiu-jitsu with Professor Williams were exactly what I needed to help separate myself from the competition. I was now a baseball player and a black belt martial artist (as well as a former football player). No one succeeds alone, so I greatly appreciated their patience, expertise, and commitment. With their help, I could channel my energy into the present and future; the past was no longer relevant. I was able to learn from a new team of coaches, good coaches who believed in me as a person. It felt great to get away from the toxicity of college sports and train in a positive environment. The ability to stay calm, breathe, and trust myself under stress would give me an advantage. Finally, I was mentally and physically ready to compete for a job somewhere in professional baseball.

Photos by Dick Cook

Hit Hard! Coach John Belskis was adamant that we always make eye contact, to *see* what we *hear*; with Dan Stringfellow (#41), Gary Higham (talking to the referee), and Nick Rasmason (#42).

"Throughout my coaching career, one of the most important lessons I believe student-athletes should learn is to expect more of themselves than others expect of them.

Brian's story represents an all too common path, from the joys of playing high school sports to the business of participating in college and professional athletics. The lessons he learned provide valuable insight for anyone who chooses to risk the journey of a non-scholarship college athlete. *Walked On* is a guide book on how maintaining high personal expectations will allow any student-athlete, parent, or coach, to overcome the "business" challenges of competitive athletics."

—

COACH JOHN BELSKIS

Head Football Coach: Downers Grove South,
Aurora Central Catholic, Minooka

Illinois High School Football Coaches
Association Hall Of Fame: 2010

Football State Champion, 8A: 2001

"Brian's career had its share of ups and downs, but he always took the downs as a challenge to make himself better. To his credit, he has done so and helped many others along the way.

Brian was a leader and led by example through hard work. I asked my players to get better each day; he accomplished that and more. It's difficult for high school kids to be role models amongst their peers, but Brian held himself to a higher standard. Brian worked as hard as he could to accomplish his dreams. If his teammates worked hard, then Brian worked harder. It didn't matter how many hits he had or how many guys he threw out, he was never satisfied and would help the team any way he could. Brian was unique because he was the type of player that coaches love to coach; he made his teammates better and his coaches, too.

Walked On is a great read at how people respond to adversity."

—

COACH PHIL FOX

Illinois High School Baseball Coaches Association Hall Of Fame: 2008

Downers Grove South High School Hall Of Fame: 2013

Instructor, Bulls/Sox Academy

Let's play two! Coach Phil Fox named me a team captain for both the summer and spring baseball seasons, adding to my perception that leaders were expected to do more.

Photos by Juli Kent

Fight for Iowa. Outside the Sun Bowl with Terry; attempting to keep big Anthony Herron (#99) away from QB Kyle McCann during the Spring Game; on the sideline against Minnesota (skinny arms don't get cold); pre-game stretch with fellow running backs Tavian Banks (#22), Michael Burger (#85), Trevor Bollers (#35), Ladell Betts (#46), Jason Baldwin (#14), Robbie Crockett (#42), and Coach Larry Holton; with my sisters, Ally and Maggie, after the Spring Game.

"Brian's honesty, passion and grit through his journey as an athlete will motivate, inspire, and encourage athletes to believe in their strengths to find happiness and success in every aspect of life.

I respect Brian's candidness in sharing his story and displaying what a true champion looks like."

—

JULIANNE SITCH

Sky Blue FC Draft Pick: 2009

Former Interim Division I Head Soccer Coach

DePaul University Scholarship Soccer Player

"Moving away from home, going to college, and meeting someone you're going to live with for the next year can fuel many emotions. This was my destiny, and there he was, Brian Kent, my new roommate. He approached me with the biggest smile and warmest greeting. At that very moment I thanked God he didn't bless me with a weirdo. Over time I came to really understand who Brian Kent was. In my eyes he was caring, honest, goofy at times, and a very hard working individual.

Having baseball as our unifying bond, he taught me that no matter the talent level, hard work supersedes all.

Till this day, from afar, he has maintained those unbelievable attributes. Along the way he became a husband and a father. That very boy I met at the University of Nebraska on Floor 7 of Harper Hall has surpassed the many great things I've already thought of him. It is an honor to be apart of this book, and through reading it, my wish is that every reader truly understands that hard work and determination created it!!!"

—

KEN HARVEY

Kansas City Royals Draft Pick: 1999

MLB All-Star: 2004

University of Nebraska Scholarship Baseball Player

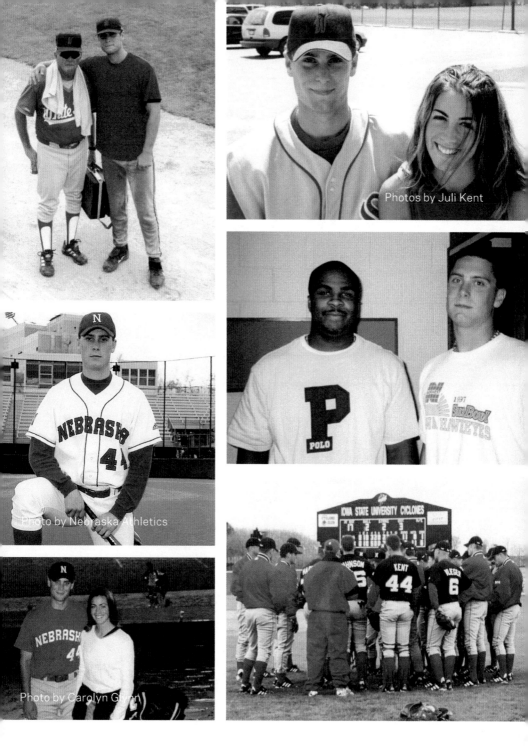

Photos by Juli Kent

Photo by Nebraska Athletics

Photo by Carolyn Glynn

There is no place like Nebraska. With Bill Slight and Jacque after Wheaton White Sox games; with Jacque at Rosenblatt Stadium; with roommate Ken Harvey at Harper Hall; inside the Big Red huddle with Brandt Vlieger (#6) and Brian Johnson (#16) at Iowa State.

Photos by Jacque Kent

Photo by Felix Lanier

The "gentle way." With Sensei Douglas Tono and Raleigh.

"Brian Kent has been a valued member of the Tohkon Judo Academy since 2007. With years of dedication and hard work Brian earned his Black Belt in Judo. To be awarded this rank at Tohkon takes tremendous commitment and respect for Judo.

Brian's sincere devotion to martial arts along with his experience as a two-sport college athlete and professional athlete has given him tremendous insight and knowledge about physical training and mental discipline.

I've had the great opportunity of not only being Brian's Judo instructor, but also his client. I am very fortunate and honored to have been trained by Brian Kent, one of the best Personal Trainers in Chicago, who got me in top physical condition which gave me a great advantage in winning the Veteran's Judo World Championships in 2010."

—

DOUGLAS TONO

President, Tohkon Judo Academy

7th Degree Black Belt, Judo

Veteran's World Champion: 2010, 2019

"I have had the privilege of not only calling Brian Kent my student but more importantly, my friend. Brian came to me with an interest in improving the ground aspects of his judo study. From day one he brought the analytical mindset of a true athlete trying to improve performance.

He possesses that special talent to not get lost in the big picture, but rather to focus on the little details that produce big effect. He's endured through hours of tough training, to gleam lessons the hard way, through effort and failure.

We have always had great conversations of sport and mindset and he gets it in a way most don't. He understands that there is no easy route to success and talent is nothing without cultivation. His experience with elite level athletics is a true asset that sets him apart from most in his field. He practices what he preaches and is a man of character. I know him as a devoted husband and father. I will always be proud to call him my friend and look forward to every time we train."

—

TONY WILLIAMS

Owner, Rebel Sport and Fitness

Black Belt, Brazilian Jiu-Jitsu

University of Wisconsin Scholarship Football Player

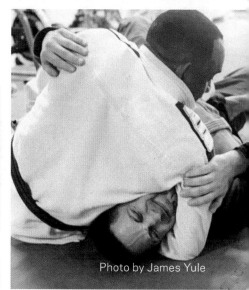

Photo by James Yule

The "gentle art." With Raleigh's favorite uncle, Professor Tony Williams.

STEPHANIE DOWELL/POST-T

RailCats catcher Brian Kent (44) stands as Joliet's Derek Kopacz
toward home plate after hitting another home run for the
JackHammers in the fourth inning Monday at U.S. Steel Yard in G

Independent league baseball. With Juli, Ally, Rusty the RailCat, Maggie, and Terry. No one
expects the catcher to bunt for a hit.

"This book narrates the unique journey that individuals go through to develop into elite level athletes.

Take a look into what makes an athlete tick, how the team environment affects an athlete's progress, and what makes an athlete excel. A must read for players, coaches, parents and the entire athletic community who are looking to get the most out of their performance!"

—

RYAN CURRY

Florida Marlins Draft Pick: 2007

Bradley University Hall Of Fame: 2019

Bradley University Scholarship Baseball Player

"I have worked with Brian Kent for over a decade, both as a co-worker and as a wingman. No one knows performance and hard work better than Brian.

I'm proud to be called his "work-wife" as well as a friend. His work ethic — both as a trainer and an athlete — inspire me to be better, daily. Brian's passion as an athlete has transcended his career to be one of the top trainers I have ever worked with. He's a black belt, former professional baseball player, Division I athlete, among other reputable accomplishments. I am honored to have such a talented co-worker and director in my corner, at On Your Mark."

—

EMILY HUTCHINS

Owner, On Your Mark Coaching and Training

Nike Master Trainer

Nike Run Club Coach

Photo by Michael Patton

Photo by Nate Anderson

#TRAINCHICAGO

Photo by Emmanuel Camacho

Just Do It. With Raleigh, Emily Hutchins, and the Nike Chicago team.

Photo by Tom Porter

Photos by Terry Kent

South side pride — Cactus League-style. With Uncle Bob and Terry, cousin Willie and Aunt Pam.

"This is a life story about the power that derives from action, hope and positivity. Brian's experiences in the world of college and professional sports are sure to resonate with any athlete.

What is unique is his ability to inspire the non-athlete — the lawyers, executives, artists, and students he works with every day. Each of us is shaped by our experiences; Brian has used his to make us see in our own lives the best of the worst; to see how the tough times and difficult experiences can bring out the best of who we are."

—

JENNIFER T. NIJMAN

Founding partner, NijmanFranzetti, LLP

Former president Chicago Bar Association

STEVEN M. SURDELL

Director of International Tax Services, Ernst & Young, LLP

Adjunct professor, Northwestern University

Baseball Card by Gary South Shore Railcats

GARY

"I CAN ACCEPT FAILURE. EVERYONE FAILS AT SOMETHING. BUT I CAN'T ACCEPT NOT TRYING."
– Michael Jordan

I had to be realistic. With my awful college stats, no major league team would dare sign me. Most college players have about 800 career at-bats; a sample size large enough to project professional success. I had 42 at-bats and hit like shit. Plus, I was coming back from rotator cuff surgery. Nothing about my history screamed, "We have to sign this guy!" While I felt I belonged at a high level, it was evident that if I were going to play professionally, I would have to start from the very bottom and claw my way up.

Independent ball, or "indy ball," is a reference to the independent minor leagues. While it is professional baseball — all players are under contract and receive a paycheck — it is its own entity and not affiliated with any parent, major league club. The season is shortened, beginning around mid-May instead of early April. The caliber of play, depending on the team, can be as high as Triple-A or as low as Rookie Ball. The roster is usually built with a handful of veteran players hanging onto their careers; some guys who were recently released from affiliated teams; and rookies out of college who went undrafted.

Fortunately, Chicagoland had three independent teams that competed in the Northern League. The Northern League, at the time, was considered to be one of the top independent leagues. The Schaumburg Flyers, Joliet JackHammers, and Gary (IN) SouthShore RailCats were all within easy driving distance of my parents house. I did not have an Arliss Michaels or an Ari Gold as my agent, so I wrote letters and made phone calls to every team in the Northern League, pleading for an opportunity. I would have gone anywhere, but my hope was to stay around Chicagoland. The feedback was consistent: Go to the Northern League tryout in Arizona.

* * * *

After 18 months of grueling physical therapy, I was medically cleared to play ball. I had been working as a substitute teacher at South, plus coaching/training with the varsity baseball team. Coach Fox and my dad allowed me to get plenty of practice reps, so I prepared the best way that I could. That 2003 South team was stacked with talent. They had three future Division I players who were all drafted out of college — Ryan Curry (Butler, Florida Marlins), Kitt Kopeck (Illinois State, Chicago Cubs), and Kevin Dubler (Illinois State, Chicago White Sox). Their youthful hunger was contagious and inspiring, and helped fuel my desire to break into pro ball.

When I arrived in Arizona, the plan regarding my tryout was simple: Do well and sign a contract. In my mind, the purpose of the tryout was for teams to find overlooked players. As a defense-oriented, left-handed hitting catcher returning from shoulder surgery, I was definitely an overlooked player. All I had to do was play well and see where it took me. But, unlike those MLB tryout camps from previous summers, there were adults at the Northern League tryout who had no business being on the field. Some looked like they hadn't played baseball since Little League — couldn't throw, couldn't catch, couldn't run. I caught a couple of bullpens where the pitcher did not throw a single strike during their tryouts. Not one! For all the Northern League coaches, managers, and scouts, there was a lot of wasted time that day. I had a good tryout — threw a 1.90, hit well, ran well — and so did another catcher. Jeb Wiseman went home with a St. Paul Saints contract; I went home with nothing. If playing well did not ensure a contract, what more could I do?

Once again, I had no team. If I had played poorly, maybe I would have ended the journey. If I felt like my skills were not up to professional standards, maybe it would have been time to find a "real job." If my arm hurt, I could justify the end. If I were overmatched, it would have been time to give it up. But, that wasn't the case. Pro baseball is not for everyone, but it most definitely was for me. I stayed hungry because I felt I was so close to signing a contract somewhere. My pop-times, post-surgery, were still under 2.0. I caught well, and I hit, too. There had to be a place for me, and right before the start of Northern League spring training, I got a call from the Schaumburg Flyers. Terry Sullivan was the head coach at nearby Lyons Township High School, and he doubled as a local Florida Marlins scout. He had coached against me and closely followed my career thereafter, staying in touch with Coach Fox and my dad. Coach Sullivan thought I deserved a chance to play, so he called Schaumburg and suggested that they invite me to their spring training. The Flyers complied and brought me in. They already had two catchers under contract, but nonetheless, it was an opportunity to compete.

In affiliated baseball, spring training is usually a month long. For independent teams, it's only two weeks. There was not much time to make an impression in Schaumburg. I held my own when the opportunities presented themselves, but still questioned my shoulder when throwing accuracy waned. We had scrimmages against Joliet and Gary, and while I was not yet the player I was pre-surgery, I was improving every day and my shoulder was pain-free. But, as the third catcher on a roster with two contracted catchers, I would probably not make the team. After the final exhibition game against Gary, I was cut. However, Billy Malone was the Gary second baseman. Billy had been my Wheaton White Sox teammate and an infielder at Robert Morris College before getting drafted by the Los Angeles Dodgers and playing a few years in their organization. I asked him to recommend me to Gary should their catching situation change.

In the meantime, I worked out for the Cook County Cheetahs and the Rockford RiverHawks, both local teams in the independent Frontier League. No contracts were offered. I felt like a terrible traveling salesman: Everywhere I went, I presented a strong product but no one wanted to buy it. It was mentally crushing to consistently come up empty. The definition of insanity is to repeat an action and expect a different result. Either I was insane in the brain or crazy like a fox, but it got me thinking hard about my baseball future. Making the most of opportunities should lead to more opportunities, but what if it doesn't? If I tried out, played well, and still didn't make it? Then what? At times, it felt like I was fighting an uphill battle on an icy hill with roller skates on my feet. I hoped my best baseball was still to come, but for who and when? I tried to focus on staying positive and being ready if I got the call. But, there were no calls. It was demoralizing to always walk away with nothing.

Truthfully, I wanted to play for the Gary SouthShore RailCats. They had a brand new ballpark and were managed by Garry Templeton (yes, Garry was the manager in Gary). Garry played 15 years in the big leagues as a shortstop, making three All-Star teams. Prior to the RailCats, he managed Triple-A for the Anaheim Angels organization. If anyone knew what it took to get to the top levels of baseball, it was Garry Templeton. A couple of weeks into the Northern League season, I got a call from Gary General Manager Roger Wexelberg. He remembered me from Schaumburg, heard good things about me from Billy Malone, and was looking to upgrade their catching position. Roger asked if I would come to Gary for a workout.

* * * *

Garry Templeton and I were the only ones on the field at U.S. Steel Yard. I remembered Garry from my Northern League tryout in Arizona, and he remembered me too. He liked what he saw both in Arizona and during my brief stint with Schaumburg. Garry wanted to know my story, so I told him the Cliffs Notes version of my college career, and that I was trying to get my confidence back post-surgery. After playing catch together, we were ready for pop-times. Garry hung out at second base while I fired throws to him from behind the plate. I was nervous as hell, and bounced a few. He effortlessly picked them out of the dirt, offering encouragement along the way. As a kid, I collected Garry Templeton's baseball cards, and now he was deciding whether or not I would make his team. It was surreal. When it was time to hit, the RailCats players began filtering onto the field, so Garry hung out behind the batting cage with hitting coach Brent Bowers. Bowers, an outfielder in his playing days, was in the big leagues with the Baltimore Orioles. Pitching coach Scott May, a big leaguer with many teams, also stopped to watch. Bench coach Joe Gates, played in the big leagues with the Chicago White Sox as a second baseman. Aside from legendary Omaha pitching coach Dan McGinn, none of my college coaches played in the big leagues, but everyone on the Gary SouthShore RailCats staff had. They had all been where I wanted to go, so I definitely needed to impress them.

Undisciplined or poorly coached hitters will use batting practice as an opportunity to club as many home runs as possible. There is zero value to it and it's a false ego boost. In Lincoln, two of Coach Anderson's finer teaching points were to approach each day with a "four-for-four attitude," and to use batting practice to hit with a purpose. The "four-for-four attitude" was about maintaining a positive mentality throughout baseball's daily failures, and hitting with a purpose put an emphasis on practicing situational hitting. We had different goals for each round of BP. The concept of practicing game-specific situations made perfect sense. While taking my first round of BP, I tried to apply both of Coach Anderson's messages: Two sacrifice bunts, two hit-and-runs, two moving the runner over to third from second base, and two getting the runner home from third with fewer than two outs — all without being told to do so.

Again, I went home with nothing, but Roger called a few days later to offer my first professional baseball contract, for $750/month. I wasn't rich, but it was a start! In addition to my throwing, Roger said that Garry had been impressed with my batting practice approach. He liked that I had a plan and was working on team-first situations that would help us win a game. While no one has a goal of playing lowly independent ball, it was a start, and it felt great to finally be wanted. It was interesting that I was good enough to play professionally for Garry Templeton but not collegiately for Dave Van Horn; further proof that one person's opinion is never final. I was assigned jersey #44 and ready to start my pro career.

The 2003 season was finally my time to show what I could do. I set a goal of waiting patiently for an opportunity, playing well, and earning a starting position. I got my first professional hits in my second career game, and played well behind the plate. I was amped to take advantage of the chance to start everyday and make up for lost college playing time. But, we quickly added veteran catcher Rene Pinto, who recently had been released from the New York Yankees organization. Rene was our starter and I was the backup. I played once a week and struggled in the role. Plus, as a team, we were bad. Our roster was a revolving door, with new guys coming in all the time. No jobs were safe. I felt I was easily expendable so I tried to do everything in my power to make Gary keep me. Every home date, I drove the Chicago Skyway to the ballpark, paying the $5 tolls to make sure I arrived early enough to hit in the cage before batting practice. I caught any pitcher who needed extra work. I always hustled. My process was sound, I just needed better results, so the new goal was to make it the full season without getting released. While I survived, I had more shitty stats (.191 average in 53 at-bats; .963 fielding percentage with 3 errors). The first season post-surgery was not my best baseball.

Compared with college baseball, pro baseball is easy. In college, everyone has classes, homework, studying, tests, quizzes, mid-terms, and finals. Factor in the baseball travel schedule and subsequent missed school, it's easy to get behind academically. There is little free time, because there is always something to catch up with. Professional baseball has no academic eligibility requirements. There is one rule for a 7pm game: 3pm arrival. So, when the game ends at 10pm until the 3pm next-day-arrival time, there are 17 uncommitted hours. That's a ton of free time, and some guys can't handle the independence. It's common to make a habit of staying out late after the game, sleeping until noon, and grabbing a Red Bull before heading to the stadium. It's easy to be lazy in such a laid-back environment. If no one preaches accountability, self-discipline is extremely important. But, as professionals and grown young men, we were expected to be responsible and make good decisions. Respecting the game was a must; some guys did and some guys didn't.

*   *   *   *

During the year, Garry Templeton proved that he would fight for me — something my college baseball coaches rarely did. On the road against the Lincoln SaltDogs, with Jacque and her family in the stands, I got run over at the plate in a collision where I was the nail. Normally, I relish these situations; anticipating this type of impact is similar to a fullback stopping a blitzing linebacker from penetrating the "A" gap. Catchers are definitely at a disadvantage — the opponent has a 90-foot head start and is running downhill; I essentially, am a stationary target. Phil Thompson's throw was coming from right field, and as I blocked home plate my vision looked to the right while the runner approached from my left. This specific instance was more comparable to a quarterback eyeing the downfield receivers as his internal clock runs out; knowing the defense is collapsing the pocket around him but not being able to actually see the edge rushers. I knew it was a bang-bang play and there could be contact, I just hoped there would be time for me to react and defend myself. There wasn't. The SaltDogs player ran through me, sending my helmet and mask flying off my head and knocking me into a backward somersault that carried me completely out of the dirt around the batter's box. It was the hardest I had ever been hit on the baseball field. He was able to separate me from home plate, but not the ball from my glove — the runner was out. My mentality was to protect the ball at all times, so I didn't mind taking one for the team.

Garry was furious — not at the collision, that's part of the game — because the guy tried to take my head off. He made no attempt to actually score; his sole intent was to blow me up. I was focused on fielding Phil's throw, so I knew that I got smashed, but not specifically how it happened. According to Garry, he came in high, as a headhunter, which went against the Garry-Templeton-baseball-code: It's okay to hit the catcher, but only in ways that Garry approved. Today, if this play against the SaltDogs had occurred in a college football game, the offender would have been ejected and suspended for "Targeting."

Channeling his inner Hammurabi, Garry ordered our pitcher to drill him in the upper back his next time up. So we did. It was a message that screamed *don't fuck with our catcher* and a reminder that Garry would always reference baseball's unwritten rules to protect his players. Later in the season, at home against Schaumburg, starting pitcher Todd George had a tough inning, giving up a handful of runs. Todd was a good pitcher, coming to Gary from the Montreal Expos organization. But in this moment, Todd and I were not aligned with pitch selection. Pre-game, we both listened to Scott May dissect the Schaumburg lineup but had different interpretations about how we were going to implement the plan. As I went out to the mound to talk to Todd, we argued over the scouting report. He started yelling and swearing at me, loud enough for people in the stands to hear. Garry immediately removed him from the game and traded him to Fargo-Moorhead shortly thereafter. It was another message reminding players of how Garry wanted the game to be played — publicly disrespecting teammates would not be tolerated. For reasons unbeknownst to me, Garry Templeton always had his light-hitting rookie catcher's back. Unofficially, I heard that Garry was building his team with players he thought would succeed in affiliated baseball; he was not as interested in daily wins and losses. He treated independent ball as a developmental league, and wanted to see his RailCats contribute at higher levels. For Garry to sign me, and keep me around, meant that he saw potential in my future (after the season ended, rookie pitchers Sazi Guthrie and Jake Upwood both signed with the San Diego Padres).

* * * *

I achieved my goal and kept my spot the entire season, even after the addition of a third catcher to our roster. The reason I stuck around, I believe, is because of my work habits. On road trips, I would wake up early to have breakfast in the hotel — usually with Garry — then go to the gym. I tried to be as professional as I knew how to be. Plus, as a backup catcher hitting under .200, I had plenty of time to think about my shitty stats. The RailCats were paying me to play baseball, not party all night. I didn't go out after games and still didn't drink alcohol. I was stressed about my performance and embarrassed by my terrible batting average, which lit up the scoreboard every time I walked to the plate. But, veterans like Tim Byrdak taught me to relax and enjoy the game. Tim was a former big league pitcher who was returning from potentially-career-ending Tommy John elbow surgery, and soon after Gary, he would be back in the big leagues. He had played at the highest level, and was now down at the lowest level. Tim stressed the importance of having fun and enjoying each day, because it could all be over at any time.

It was great advice.

Photo by San Angelo Colts

7

SAN ANGELO

"SET YOUR GOALS HIGH, AND DON'T STOP UNTIL YOU GET THERE."

– Bo Jackson

After getting released from Gary in the off-season, I needed to find a new team. While my first year in pro ball was a good experience, I still had poor offensive stats. My goal was to get signed by a major league team, and that wasn't going to happen with a batting average less than my bodyweight. Offensively, my college seasons plus Gary was a combined .157 batting average (14 for 89). Awful. But, I did not consider myself to be a shitty hitter. I could hit, but hadn't been hitting. I hoped there was a difference. I needed more playing time to show what I could do on an everyday basis. Or, I needed to play better in limited opportunities. Either way, there were times I played well, and times I did not. In baseball, guys who found consistency moved up; guys who were inconsistent went home.

In the early spring of 2004, I was invited to a Boston Red Sox workout for independent league players. I flew to Fort Myers, Florida, home of the Red Sox spring training facility.

Like previous MLB workouts, I performed well. No contracts were offered, but it was a reminder that I belonged. Here was the problem: I passed the eyeball test, but failed the background check. There were too many questions about my past to seriously consider signing me. But, I decided that as long as I had the physical tools to play baseball at a professional level, I would pursue it. Also in my favor: Left-handed hitting catchers will always be in high demand. It's a rare combination, because most catchers hit right-handed. The two fastest routes to the big leagues are to be a left-handed pitcher or a left-handed hitting catcher. If I played any other position, or hit right-handed, it would have been harder to stand out. But, I figured that if I could just hit around .250, my defensive skills might carry me to the next level.

Right before the beginning of the 2004 Northern League season, I went to Silver Cross Field for a Joliet JackHammers tryout. Joliet was managed by Jeff Isom — his first year in Joliet — and they were looking for a catcher. My tryout was solid; I threw, ran, and hit well. But, unlike previous tryouts, Joliet offered me a contract on site! I signed for $800/month. It was perfect. I was still in the Northern League, still in Chicagoland, and still fighting to move up. As long as I had a heartbeat, I had a chance. Jeff explained that, similar to Gary, my job was to be the backup catcher. Now, I had to play better in this defined role.

But, a week into Joliet spring training, Jeff called me into his office. Based on past conversations with coaches behind closed doors, I knew this was bad. He informed me that I was being released for financial reasons. Somehow, my $800/month was putting the JackHammers over their Northern League-mandated salary cap, so my contract was voided and I was now off the team. In the interim, Joliet would have only one catcher, and use an outfielder as the emergency backup. The business of baseball was new for me, but I was definitely one of the lowest-paid guys on the roster, and in the league. Did my contract really impact JackHammer economics? Getting released over $800/month was a brand new baseball low. The game was severely testing my patience.

*   *   *   *

The worst part about getting released from Joliet was that it was not performance-based. If I played poorly, and it was clear I was overmatched and did not belong, then I would understand not making the team. Playing like shit makes personnel decisions easy. Basically, players will play themselves on or off the team. I still believed in my ability and stayed extremely motivated. I had just turned 25 years-old, so my window to compete was rapidly closing. But, I could still pop it to second base in under two seconds and swing it from the left side. I was mentally willing to keep fighting and grinding.

Much like my transition from Schaumburg to Gary, every roster in the Northern League was set, so I had to wait. With the season just starting, no one was going to make any new personnel decisions. From the outside, all I could do was stay ready. Still without an agent, once a week, I called every team in the league, asking for consideration should their catching situation change. Finally, a few weeks into June, the Lincoln SaltDogs offered an atypical proposition. Manager Tim Johnson was looking to make a roster move, but wasn't sure when. They wanted me as a non-roster player, to basically be on stand-by for when they made a decision. I would work out with the team; but not be on the team. I would practice; but not play. It sounded like my redshirt year in Iowa City, and not an ideal situation. But, the SaltDogs were the only team to call me back. I had no other baseball options.

With my life packed into the Kent family Chevy Cavalier (after the Escort died Terry and Juli replaced it with a Cavalier), I drove back to Lincoln. The gift and the curse of an eight-hour solo car ride is that it offered plenty of time to think. If the SaltDogs had a contract waiting for me, with some version of a "normal" baseball season, making this decision would have been easy. But, nothing was guaranteed. There was a chance I could get there and they would not make any roster moves. Then what would I do? Ultimately, I realized that as a walk-on and an undrafted free agent playing independent league baseball, I had to eat many shit sandwiches on my journey to the top. This path toward signing with a major league team was not linear, but a loop-de-loop roller coaster, with more downs than ups. It was a test from the universe to see if I *really* wanted to make it in baseball. Plus, being back in Lincoln meant the chance of bumping into my old Nebraska coaches, as the Huskers and SaltDogs shared the same facility at brand new Haymarket Park. What would I say if I saw them? Would I remain calm? Or calm like a bomb? Into July, I was still on retainer and the season was almost half over. When Tim asked to see me in his office, I figured my short time with the SaltDogs was over. I was mentally prepared to be sent home and already trying to figure out what my next life steps would be. However, he asked if I would be interested in playing for the San Angelo (TX) Colts, of the independent Central League. Tim didn't know what would happen with the SaltDogs' catching situation, so he thought a change of scenery might give me something stable. San Angelo needed a catcher, and I needed a job. I signed the contract for $600/month. I still wasn't rich, but at least it was something. The Central League had teams in Texas, Louisiana, Mississippi, and Florida — all parts of the country known for their sweltering summers.

*   *   *   *

It was more than 800 miles from Lincoln to San Angelo, and I hoped my car could physically make it — with my baseball luck, the Cavalier would break down in the middle of Amarillo and I would be sliced up by Leatherhead from the Texas Chainsaw Massacre. Clearly, I had extra time to think during this trip. It was hard to stay sane during the 13-hour ride, but I needed to arrive in San Angelo with the proper mindset. It was imperative that I seamlessly transition into playing well. On the drive, I entertained myself by practicing a Southern accent, hoping to perfect my Texas twang. *Y'all from around here?* In college, we played Texas, Texas A&M, Texas Tech, Baylor, and Rice. I had been to El Paso for the Sun Bowl. So, I was slightly familiar with the Texas culture. Still, the drive to San Angelo was the most I had ever driven in my life. Cruising through Nebraska, Kansas, Oklahoma, and into Texas went right through the heart of the Big XII Conference. I recognized the landscape, because I had been there before. The more the scenery changed, the more it stayed the same.

The San Angelo Colts were led by rookie manager Toby Rumfield. The previous year, I had played against Toby when he was with the Fargo-Moorhead RedHawks. At 31 years-old, he was a young manager but a baseball-lifer with 13 seasons of minor league playing experience. Toby was straight with me: Playing well equals playing more. The 2004 season was half over by the time I arrived in San Angelo, and I was itching to compete. When I got my chance to play, I took advantage. I split time initially, but played myself into catching more games than I sat. Finally, this was the opportunity I had patiently waited for: A chance to earn consistent playing time and produce accordingly. As a rhythm sport, baseball is unusually cruel. Inconsistent rhythm equals inconsistent performance. Regular playing time usually leads to an offensive rhythm, which leads to consistent performance. In Gary, I had been fighting the play-once-a-week battle and never got into a rhythm. In San Angelo, I got a chance to find a rhythm and played my way into the lineup. Making the most of opportunities leads to more opportunities.

Midway through the second half of our season, the Colts made major changes. Toby resigned as the manager, but stayed on as a player. John Harris became our new manager and traded for a new catcher, Andrew York. He named York the starter, while I found my way back to the bench. Demoted to backup duties, my batting average began to drop. I had a really hard time with John's decision. After all these years of chasing playing time, I finally found it in San Angelo. I played well, and Toby had rewarded me. Then, WHAM!, due to factors outside my control, I was on the bench. Terry and his brother Bob, were planning to fly from Chicago to watch me play. They had made these plans when I was the starting catcher, but now, what was the point to watch me sit on the San Angelo bench? I told them to cancel the trip. The season was close to over, and I was sick of the bullshit and ready to ask for my release from the team. One late night in a San Angelo bar, pitchers Dave Therneau and Chad Johnson talked me out of it.

By chance, Dave Therneau and I worked out together when we were in Omaha. I was a damaged catcher; he was a damaged pitcher. I was coming back from shoulder surgery; he was coming back from Tommy John elbow surgery. Dave would throw me BP; I would catch his bullpens. Neither one of us was at our best when we met, but he was way more established. A native Texan, Dave pitched at Texas Tech, was drafted by the Cincinnati Reds, and got up to Triple-A before being injured. We played against each other the previous year when he was with Schaumburg. Now, as teammates, Dave also doubled as the Colts' pitching coach (and is currently the associate head coach at Stetson University). He explained to me that asking for a release from my contract is comparable to a baseball Scarlet Letter. No team wants the drama of a player who asked for his release from an independent league team — no matter the reason. He told me to start acting like a man and to finish the year strong.

I trusted Dave and decided to suck it up. I had not played myself out of a job, so I had to make the best of this situation. Baseball can be such a mind-fuck, so I needed to be mentally tougher and not let outside decisions distract me from larger goals. I made a late season commitment to finishing the season with a batting average of .250. I had been playing great defensively, only making one error the whole year. With a .994 fielding percentage combined with a left-handed .250 batting average, I might earn some interest from affiliated teams. Heading into the final game of the 2004 season — which I was penciled into the starting lineup — I needed to go 1-3 to finish at .250. But, the baseball gods had other plans and the game was rained out. (August rain in West Central Texas? Come on!) Since the Central League champion had already been crowned, our game was meaningless and not rescheduled. I finished the year hitting .246 (17 for 69).

*   *   *   *

As I drove home to Chicago, I was proud that I had stuck it out. These two years of independent ball had tested my patience, my mental toughness, and my personal grit. They were an extension of college, where I got a taste but was far from satisfied. The lifestyle was ridiculously unglamorous and my bank account was practically empty. I had played sparingly, with spurts of consistency surrounded by longer bouts of inactivity. Whether it was a bus ride from Gary to Winnipeg, or from San Angelo to Pensacola, there was plenty of time for reflection. *Did I really want to do this?* During those bus rides to nowhere, I passed the hours by reading many books about martial art philosophy. I kept asking myself if I was following the right path. The truth was, I loved baseball and I loved being a baseball player. I loved proving myself right. My mind was in the big leagues, but my body was in the independent leagues. I was not playing at the professional level where I wanted to be, but I had come a long way from those moments of not knowing if I would ever play again. I did not want to continue my career in the independent leagues, but no major league teams were calling.

I was offered a job playing in the Mexican Liga Norde de Señora, but the pay could not cover my rent. Simply, I could not afford to play. Now in my mid-20s, I had to make some hard, adult decisions regarding my future. My body was healthy and I made improvements in my mental game. I had two seasons of pro ball under my belt, but no team. It looked like baseball was over.

Photo by Mike Hammer

TRAIN

**"WHEN THE MIND IS ALLOWED TO RELAX,
INSPIRATION OFTEN FOLLOWS."**

– Phil Jackson

When I graduated from Omaha, I had no backup career plan. It was baseball or nothing: There was no Plan B. My English degree was nice to have, but I didn't want a real job; I wanted a baseball job. I liked having a piece of paper that said I completed college, but had no idea what English majors do for work, so I started substitute teaching at South. Since Terry was a teacher and Juli was a CPR instructor, I thought teaching might be in the Kent blood. I also enrolled in graduate courses at DePaul University, to earn a Master's of Education. But, my heart was never in it. While I enjoyed coaching, I lacked enthusiasm for teaching English and going to school. Terry came home from practice and spent a good chunk of his evenings grading homework — that life wasn't for me. I stopped attending DePaul after two quarters.

My two deepest passions were baseball and getting ready for baseball. I loved baseball training, just like I loved football training. I was lucky to have had great strength coaches throughout college. From Paul Longo and Parker Wildeman in Iowa City, to Lacey Degnan and Shaun Huls in Lincoln, and Dave Noonan and Quinn Peterson in Omaha — these were big names that continued to be industry leaders. There was a direct correlation between weight room commitment and on-field performance. The off-season process helped determine the in-season outcome. Guys who worked hard and got bigger, stronger, and faster usually played better. I was sold on its simplicity. Also, weights always spoke the truth. Either the weight was moved for a full repetition, or it wasn't. The weight room was the ultimate bullshit-free proving ground.

In Omaha, sandwiched between school, baseball, and shoulder rehab, I had a job as the weight room supervisor in the campus rec center. The pay was crap, but I liked working in the gym. Being a college strength coach did not appeal to me — I did not have the education and college-town life held little appeal. There had to be another way, so I looked into personal training. I never had a trainer nor did I know anyone that was a trainer, but I was interested in creating a solid path in a field that I was passionate about. I liked helping people and thought I could leverage my teaching experience into the fitness industry. I thought that sports and martial arts gave me a credible background, and what I lacked in formal education, I made up for in practical application.

*   *   *   *

Rather than start small with a neighborhood gym, I wanted to work in the Loop. To me, working in downtown Chicago was the "major leagues" for professionals. I picked Crunch Fitness, located in historic Marina City. Right away, it was clear that personal training was not just about giving a good workout — there were a million other components. In addition to designing a specific-to-the-client program, trainers were responsible for selling training packages, building and managing a business, professional development, achieving monthly monetary goals, and providing elite customer service. The only part of the job description I understood was that each client deserved a personalized workout. Football players and baseball players trained differently, due to the different demands of their sport. It made sense that clients should train differently too, based on their specific needs. But, I needed to learn a lot more if I was going to succeed in the fitness industry.

Fortunately, I was hired by James Bach. Before becoming the Crunch Fitness regional personal training director for Chicago and Atlanta, James was the captain of his baseball team at Northern Illinois University and a two-sport captain at Lane Tech College Prep on Chicago's north side. He was a martial artist and a published poet. What he wasn't, was some meathead who could only find work in a gym. He and I connected right away. As a trainer, he saw the body from a completely different lens. He quickly earned my trust and I held him in equal regard to my college strength coaches. James took the time to develop and prepare me for the industry. He devoted many hours teaching, answering questions, and guiding my career, while encouraging me to be myself. It was great to have a coach personally invest in me.

Privately, I feared I would be at an educational disadvantage compared with my colleagues. Many trainers had degrees in exercise science or kinesiology, while mine was in English. Also, I knew nothing about business or sales, so I had to catch up in all three phases. I soon learned there was no correlation between education and performance. I saw some highly educated trainers who were irritatingly lazy, just as I saw some trainers without college degrees have a consistent clientele. There were trainers with amazing bodies — who looked like they knew what they were doing — who were awful trainers. There were trainers with regular bodies — who *did not* look like they knew what they were doing — who were quite knowledgeable. This industry was fickle and difficult to predict. There were many paths to success, so I needed to find my niche.

James talked about how the "hustle" on the baseball field was the same "hustle" in the gym. The principles were identical. An athlete truism is that *hustle never goes into a slump* and that *hustle requires no talent*. Sports can be unforgivingly random, with the outcome often out of the athlete's control. But, preparation and process is always under our control. No matter the score or the individual statistics, we are all in charge of our effort level. As a catcher, I was always hustling to back up throws to first base, or to beat out an infield single. As a fullback, I was always hustling for more yards, or to block through the whistle. Sports, training, business, and life were all the same: More hustle leads to more success. My clientele grew not because I was the best, most educated trainer. It grew because I was willing to put in the work, to embrace the grind. Crunch's primetime hours were before-work, mid-day, and after-work. It was common to be in the gym from 5am until 8pm. The lifestyle was not for everybody, but trainers who wanted to hustle were rewarded. Plus, wearing sweatpants to "the office" while training interesting people seemed like a great career choice — aside from baseball.

Realistically, I was built for this. As a college athlete, long work days were the norm. We were conditioned for an all-day-everyday lifestyle. I was used to waking up early, having to perform through a full day of physical and mental commitments, and getting to bed late. In this industry, athletes had a distinct advantage because, simply, we were used to such a heavy workload. The best part was that now, I was getting paid for it. Plus, catchers and fullbacks are the hardest working guys on the team. I liked to hustle and bust my ass, all I had to do was apply myself in the same way.

*　　*　　*　　*

Initially, one of the main obstacles to my success was my insecurity around talking to new people. I am not naturally a "chatty" person, so I had to work hard at the art of conversation. James helped me get comfortable by suggesting I talk to clients as I would talk with friends or teammates; without, you know, all the swearing and ass-slapping. He also recommended keeping the focus on the client. As trainers, James explained, we were the supporting cast. Again, this perfectly fit my background. On the field, both my positions were the epitome of supporting cast. As a catcher, it was my job to help the pitcher. As a fullback, it was my job to help the tailback. I was always the helper. Now, as a trainer, it was my job to help the client.

I was also responsible for building my own clientele. One of my personality flaws is that I preferred to *show* people what I could do, instead of *tell* them. By nature, I am a doer, not a talker. It's been my experience that people who *talk* the most *do* the least. Unfortunately, when it came time to meeting with a prospective client, I had to *talk* my way into a chance to *show* them. As a kid, I had the Ryne Sandberg "Speak Softly and Carry a Big Stick" Nike poster in my bedroom, but Ryno's advice wasn't going to help now. James wanted me to be better at explaining the process; to use words — and my English degree — as a method to get people excited about the workout. Telling them what would happen before it actually happened enhanced credibility. It also showed professionalism by being confident in my methods and my actions. It was exactly the same confidence needed to walk out to the mound, and tell my pitcher how we were going to attack a hitter. If I said slider-away-followed-by-sinker-in, and it worked, I looked like a genius. If I told a client that applying self-myofascial release to their quadriceps would help their knees feel better, and it worked, I also looked like a genius.

Working with clients was very similar to working with pitchers. Developing a strong relationship and establishing rapport was important. If a pitcher trusted me, he would throw that 1-2 curve ball in the dirt because he knew that I would block it. If a client trusted me, (s)he knew I would select exercises that put them in a position to succeed. Like any good coach, I could get more out of their abilities if they believed in me and they knew I believed in them. As a catcher, it was my job to design an effective, yet adjustable game plan. I would call different pitches depending on the strengths and weaknesses of the individual pitcher. As a trainer, programming for clients was the same skill. I would have a plan and if it worked, stick with it. Or, we would modify the program based on the results. To be successful, the plan needed to be flexible.

*   *   *   *

In Lincoln, John Cole was one of my best workout partners. His versatility as a second baseman and outfielder would eventually attract the Seattle Mariners, who selected him in the 5th round of the 2001 draft. We pushed each other hard and made each other better. But, other than John, I preferred to train alone. I was never in one place long enough to develop rapport with a consistent training partner, so I usually went solo. I could always motivate myself, but as the saying goes, we are stronger together than we are alone. At Crunch, I had a whole new team of workout buddies, all with different specialties. In addition to James, Mike Bodziach was a football player and MMA fighter. Justin Brookes was a track athlete. Gabe Caldwell and Nate Cook were baseball players. Joey Thurman was a hockey player. Tony Espana, Ryan

Mark, and Donell Watts were just strong as fuck. Annette Fiscelli and Emily Hutchins were endurance athletes. Jenn Hogg and Lois Miller were sport aerobic competitors. Prima Pongspikul and Matt Praeuner were martial artists. We all brought different backgrounds and ideas to the workouts and pushed each other to get better.

I was never one of the strongest or fastest guys on any team, including South. I had only trained athletically, which was for performance rather than vanity. I was good at hang cleans and squats, but terrible at bench press and bicep curls. At Crunch, I had new teammates to help find my weaknesses, and implement a plan to strengthen them. James suggested that I add a certification from the National Academy of Sports Medicine (NASM). NASM used their Optimal Performance Training Model, which had three pillars: Stability, Strength, and Power. When I attended the NASM seminar, the instructors encouraged audience participation, so I volunteered. In front of a packed house at the Donald E Stephens Convention Center, I was asked to demonstrate a bodyweight, single-leg squat, part of the NASM movement assessment. It looked simple enough, so with all eyes on me, I tried to squat down on one leg. Awful balance combined with a shaky squat pattern resulted in a miserably failed test. I was shocked. Here I was, a (low-level) professional athlete, who had spent his life in a squat or crouched position. How was I unable to squat on one leg?

Clearly, if I failed a movement assessment I thought I would easily pass, I needed help in other areas, too. I made it my mission to apply the NASM principles to my own body. Honestly, I had terrible Stability, average Strength, and good Power. As the foundation of all movement, Stability was fundamentally important as the base for Strength and Power. All structures built on a poor foundation will crumble, including bodies. Strength and Power will never reach their maximal potential with poor Stability. Now that I had this information, it was time to apply it. If my athletic career had, thus far, lacked Stability, how good could I be if I strengthened my greatest weakness? What other gains could I unlock by just having a better base? It seemed that my best self was yet to come.

*   *   *   *

I worked on my weaknesses and saw visual changes in my physique. Due to genetics and years of heavy squats, I always had big legs and a big ass. Traditionally, shopping for pants was always a nightmare as my genes were hard to fit into jeans. But, my quads were rock hard and my butt was soft and squishy, like a giant pillow. Working through the NASM principles, I went back to those single-leg bodyweight squats. With all my weight on one leg, my big booty finally started to help out. Instead of having my weight on the balls of my feet — as I would on the field — I pushed through my heels, instantly activating my posterior chain. Immediately, my squat pattern improved and became more efficient as my glutes joined my quads as the primary movers. Finally, after years of being dormant, my big ass learned how to work!

While the Universities of Iowa and Nebraska had great strength and conditioning coaches, much of their team programming fell into the Strength and Power categories. There was little Stability work, which, not surprisingly, was my weakest link. Realizing this was my greatest area for improvement, I put myself through full-body Stability work. My upper and lower body were always doing everything with either one hand or one leg. By forcing each side to work independently, I could focus on any left-side or right-side discrepancies. The weaknesses were immediately evident, but progress was imminent. The human body is extremely adaptable, meaning it quickly adjusts to any stimulus placed upon it. Stability training was brand new for me. All the exercises were familiar, but their execution was different. I was quickly becoming the strongest version of myself, simply by solidifying my physical foundation.

My motivation to improve was high, but crushing my new enthusiasm was the thought that baseball was over and my strongest body would never have a chance to compete.

*   *   *   *

One of the perks of being affiliated with a downtown gym was that its location attracted high level professionals. Crunch was attached to the House of Blues Hotel — which often hosted concerts and various performances — so it was normal to see celebrities. Rappers Common and 50 Cent came in to lift weights, rockers Linkin Park grabbed shots of wheat grass from the juice bar, and boxing champion

Floyd Mayweather came in with his monstrous bodyguards, to name a few. But, the personality that influenced me the most was Steve Trout.

In 1976, Steve Trout was a first round draft pick of the White Sox out of local Thornwood High School in South Holland, IL. As a left-hander, Steve pitched 12 years in the big leagues with four teams, but I mainly remember his baseball cards from the White Sox and Cubs. Somehow, he had developed a relationship with James and was a frequent presence around the gym. Steve was a friendly guy with years of baseball stories.

One night, Steve joined the Crunch trainers for dinner at Fogo de Chão, with plans to grab drinks afterward at Ghost Bar, then one of Chicago's swankiest establishments. On the way to the bar — our stomachs stuffed with meat — Steve and I rode together and talked baseball, from the dynamic between pitchers and catchers to how cool it was for him to play with both the Cubs and White Sox. Steve started in the big leagues at 20 years-old, and essentially matured into an adult in major league clubhouses. He was a wealth of knowledge in baseball and life, and years later, would even make an infamous appearance at my bachelor party. But, that story is for another time...

As we pulled up to Ghost Bar, I observed the patrons entering and leaving and thought I may have been underdressed, which absolutely stressed me out. These people were dressed for a nice evening; I was dressed a bit more... casual. One of my social fears is not being appropriately dressed, and I thought the heavily-muscled bouncers might turn me away at the door. *Sorry kid, come back when you can dress like an adult.* As I meekly showed my ID, I was mentally making this situation to be much worse that it actually was. Negative self-talk allowed my confidence to plummet, and I slowly shuffled through the doors and peeked around to locate our friends, who had already arrived. Steve, with his powers of big league observance, must have noticed a change in my energy and simply wouldn't allow me to behave in this way. He grabbed me by the shoulder and dropped some veteran knowledge to help his rookie catcher:

ST: Whoa, stop. You can't walk in here like that.
Me: What?
ST: Yeah, you gotta walk in here like you've got the biggest dick in the room.
Me: What?
ST: Here, watch me.

Steve proceeded to shove me aside and strut into the bar like a man injected with confidence; presumably like a man who did have the biggest dick in the room. With a huge smile on his face, he waved to people who did not wave back to him, greeted total strangers like he'd known them for years, and generally behaved like the mayor of Ghost Bar. Throughout his career, Steve had worked rooms like this for years, and his attitude and actions were contagious. He was extremely likable and comfortable in this environment, while I looked like an outcast standing alone in the back of the room. It was clear which one of us was a seasoned social veteran. Like a pitcher on the mound, he was in his own world — completely immersed with his performance and indifferent to the crowd's reaction. But, in the moment, Steve taught me a valuable lesson. Big league confidence was not just limited to the field — it was also a lifestyle and a skill that could be learned.

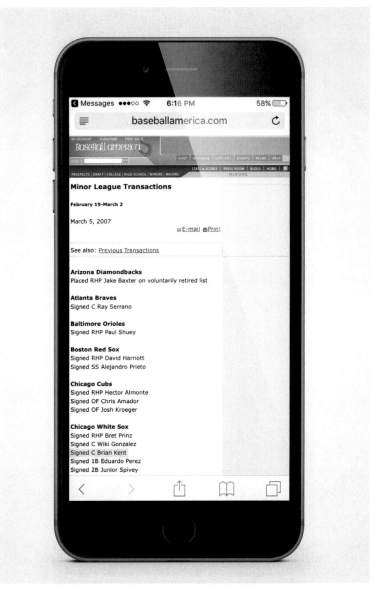

Thank you *Baseball America*, for documenting minor league transactions.

SOUTH SIDE

**"IT'S NOT WHAT YOU ACHIEVE,
IT'S WHAT YOU OVERCOME. THAT'S
WHAT DEFINES YOUR CAREER."**

– Carlton Fisk

Baseball was over. That's right, I was out of the game in 2005 and 2006. At 25 years-old, my career was done. It was not by design; I never officially "retired," but I had to be practical. Being a Major League Baseball player, or being assigned to an MLB minor league affiliate, was not in my future, and I had to accept that I fell short of achieving a lifelong goal. The pursuit of next-level athletics began in Iowa City and ended in San Angelo. Those in-between years were filled with plenty of blood, sweat, and tears, but I did not achieve my goal. I was happy to make every sacrifice had it led to the outcome I desired. But, without the ending I was fighting for, it felt incomplete. The chance to sign with a major league organization had passed me by. It was difficult to acknowledge, because I prided myself on finishing everything I started (well, aside from grad school at DePaul).

Crunch provided — for the first time in my life — consistent paychecks. Throughout college and my time in the independent leagues, I had no money. None. There were times when I had to calculate the priority: Putting gas in my car or eating lunch. In Lincoln, I once took Jacque to dinner for her birthday, but could only pay for one of us. I didn't eat that night. I was tired of being broke and having student loan officers calling me all the time. Personal training was a way to anchor my present with a career that would help build a future. My sports work ethic transferred seamlessly into the gym, and I enjoyed quick success. In time, I became an elite level trainer with a deep client roster, and was even featured in *Chicago Magazine*. It was the perfect transition away from the game. I still loved baseball, but it was my past. It felt strange going to a White Sox or a Cubs game as a fan. I had always envisioned myself on the field, but now, I sat in the stands and munched hot dogs like everybody else.

My personal workouts were great, and I trained myself to focus on areas in which I was weak. Before, I would have cared how much weight I was lifting, now I was concerned with recruiting the proper muscles to execute the technique. I tried to simplify the focus: If a movement was difficult for me, I worked on it until it became easier. There was always something to improve upon, and my body responded well to the variety. I was stable, strong, and a more well-rounded athlete than ever before. In addition, I learned how to eat cleaner. Nutrition had been a weakness for many years, and as a fitness professional, claiming ignorance was unacceptable. Dr. Jason Godo is a chiropractic physician trained in applied kinesiology and James invited him to Crunch for continuing-education workshops. Dr. Godo helped me understand how to eat smarter: Increasing fruits and vegetables, decreasing dairy products, and gain a better overall awareness of what went into my mouth. I was pleased with the results and loved training and eating for better performance.

*　*　*　*

In Chicago, baseball is a hot topic. While everyone cheers for Da Bears, Bulls, and Blackhawks, the city is divided between its two MLB teams: The Cubs and the White Sox. Everyone picks their team — or has their team picked for them — at birth. While the gray jerseys of both teams read "Chicago," Chicagoans can cheer for the North Side or the South Side, but not for both sides. Period. Year-round teasing from each fan base is expected, as the North Side and South Side love to mock each other. Thick skin is a prerequisite for all Chicago baseball fans, and the worst jabs are usually made by closest friends and family. My family and friends were split between the Cubs and White Sox, which meant relentless shit-talking. I had grown up a Cubs fan, but quit them after they lost to the Florida Marlins in the 2003 NLCS. Like many Chicagoans, I was heartbroken. Before 2016, Cubs fans traditionally had a lifetime of painful memories, and I was done with it. That 2003 loss (they were five outs away from the World Series) came after my season in Gary, on the heels of my surgery and college career. I was in a bad mental place, and the Cubs made it worse. While I would never irrationally switch allegiances and cheer for the evil White Sox, they started to steal my attention. In 2004, the White Sox hired Ozzie Guillen as their manager, and he brought a South Side swagger that Chicagoans adored. In 2005, that swagger helped the White Sox win the World Series for the first time in 88 years. In a short time, Ozzie joined mustachioed Chicago coaching legends like Mike Ditka and Phil Jackson as owners of world championship rings.

Ozzie made the White Sox locally important and nationally relevant. They were a good team and fun to watch. He was always talking crazy, but the fundamentals of "Ozzie Ball" were effective. Hustling and grinding are rooted into Chicago's bedrock, and the White Sox represented these traits. My grandfather, Irving, a lifelong White Sox fan, loved that the South Siders were finally winning. Bill Slight, another lifelong White Sox fan, loved that the White Sox won the World Series before the Cubs. Ozzie had the perfect personality to attract all types of eyes, and I started watching White Sox games because Ozzie's passion made them interesting. Truthfully, I hoped he would get ejected and unleash an ESPN-worthy tirade on some poor umpire. I did not consider myself to be a White Sox fan, but I liked watching winning baseball — something rarely seen in Chicago. Plus, after sweeping the 2005 World Series, the White Sox were the darlings of Chicago and a premier organization.

*   *   *   *

Around the start of the 2006 season, David Wilder became a member at Crunch Fitness. Sales rep Doug Collins (identical name as the former Bulls head coach, but not the same person) told me that some "White Sox scout" had just joined the gym. When I looked him up, David was not just some scout, he was the senior director of player personnel. *Whoa.* David was one of general manager Kenny Williams' top guys; someone who was being groomed as a future hotshot GM. In the White Sox front office hierarchy, he was an important man. Years before, when I needed to find a team, this could have been a dream scenario. Now, when I was out of the game, I was in the same gym as a White Sox decision-maker with the power to sign anyone he wanted. I was almost 27 years-old, and hadn't thrown a ball or swung a bat in two years. What was I supposed to do with this information? Even in my "advanced years" as a ballplayer, I would love to play for the hometown White Sox. I wanted to talk with him, but what would I say?

I saw David in the gym whenever the White Sox were in town, and it felt stereotypically like being around the girl of my dreams; a girl that was oblivious to my interest. I would get nervous and sweaty, stare at my shoes, mumble hello, but say nothing else. Then I would curse in disgust, knowing I had blown an opportunity to make a positive impression. I had to sell myself for a chance to play, but was unsure how to begin. What was the proper etiquette? Should I interrupt his workout? Start an awkward conversation while he undresses in the locker room? Follow him into the bathroom, and while he's peeing, ask for a White Sox job? It took months to formulate a plan. Without appearing to be a desperate amateur, how could I tell David that playing for the

White Sox would be a dream come true? If I finally found the balls to ask him for a chance, then what if he said no? What if David said I'm too old? What if he looked up my career stats and laughed in my face? What if he called Coach Van Horn? Could my fragile male ego handle rejection from David Wilder, a.k.a. the girl of my dreams?

I racked my brain all summer trying to figure it out. While Crunch helped develop my interpersonal skills, this conversation was way too important to fuck up. As I prepared to ask for a miracle, I practiced the various ways our dialogue could run. There was a 50/50 chance David would be interested in what I had to say. I didn't like those coin-flip odds, but my odds were zero if I said nothing. Aside from throwing a baseball across the gym to catch David's attention, I had to speak up. It was the only option. Finally, in late September, I cornered David next to the squat rack. It was time to go all in. In my RailCats Baseball T-shirt, I summoned the courage to start the most important conversation of my professional life. Here is my recollection of our discussion:

Me: Hi David!
DW: Hey Brian. Nice shirt, did you play in Gary?
Me: Yes sir, for Garry Templeton.
DW: 'Tempy' is a good guy. What position do you play?
Me: Catcher.
DW: Yeah? Can you catch?
Me: Yes sir.
DW: Yeah? Can you hit?
Me: Yes sir. I'm a left-handed hitter.

DW: Left-handed hitting catcher? Do you still play?

Me: Not since 2004. But I know I still can because it's all I've ever wanted to do.

DW: Hmm...would you want to come to camp with the White Sox next year?

Me: Wow. Yes sir!

Holy fucking shit! That was it. All my stress from thinking about this conversation was overrated, as he genuinely offered to help me. The whole exchange lasted 30 seconds and after our talk, I never saw him at Crunch again. Now, part of me thought this was a nice gesture with no follow through, but I was going to be ready just in case. Besides, if David was legit and I was unprepared for an opportunity to play with the *Chicago White Sox*, I could *never* forgive myself. *Never*. Still, I told no one. It would be premature to make this announcement after one conversation. Hell, I didn't even have a contract. A verbal agreement? No one would believe me anyway. But, I started secretly preparing as if I would be heading to Arizona. Who cared if I had been out of baseball for two years? That's two years of less mileage on my shoulder and knees. Plus, I had already missed two years of college baseball, so if anybody could mentally handle some ring rust, it was me. Right?

When I wasn't training clients, I spent the end of 2006 focused on being an athletic catcher. In addition to getting in baseball-specific shape, I cross-trained by borrowing from other sports and applied everything I had learned as a trainer. I boxed the speed bag for hand-eye coordination; ran

300-yard shuttles for mental toughness; did DB snatches for power; and medicine ball complexes for core strength. I wanted the White Sox to have the best version of me — to show my evolution as a ballplayer — and prepared the best way I knew how. But, I also had to get creative. I did not have a consistent partner to play catch with, so in my loft apartment, I threw a rubber ball off the brick wall 100 times. I would pick out a specific brick, let it rip, and hope that the rebound didn't break anything. My neighbors in the South Loop probably hated me, as I played catch with myself multiple times per week. I took hundreds of swings in the open space of my front room, visualizing game-specific situations, and staying calm. (Often, the CTA Orange or Green Line would stop on the tracks right outside my window. I'm sure the passengers stuck on the train, looking through their window and into mine, witnessed a crazy person swinging a baseball bat at an imaginary ball.) I practiced everything in my mind and tried to stay focused amidst the excitement. As the calendar year turned to 2007, there had been no further communication. Truthfully, I lost faith. *David was just being polite, he probably doesn't even remember me.*

*   *   *   *

One cold, early-February night, I fell asleep on the train while on my way to Lions Martial Arts. My phone rang and a never-before-seen 480 area code popped up on the screen. Not recognizing the phone number, I did not answer the call — which quickly developed into a new voicemail. When I listened to the message, the voice on the other end belonged to…

David Wilder! I instantly jumped up like someone lit my ass on fire. In the recording, David asked if I was still serious about playing with the Chicago White Sox. In my mind, I screamed like a 12 year-old girl at a Justin Bieber concert. Before David could change his mind, I immediately called him back, jamming the phone through my ear to make sure I accurately heard his every word against the backdrop of the noisy train. Over the phone, I tried to control my emotions and project confidence and professionalism. For David, I answered, "yes sir." For myself, I experienced a jolt of personal pride and immense confidence; my baseball demons were instantly eliminated by the South Side Hitmen.

The next day, David faxed me a free agent, minor league deal with the Chicago White Sox. At the time, signing the contract for $1,200/month was the greatest moment of my life. I can still recall the excitement and energy surging through my veins as I put pen to paper; I had never experienced a euphoria like it. The Kents were ecstatic. My journey had validation. All the physical and emotional scars of giving my life to the game were worth it. Finally, this was the opportunity to prove myself with a MLB organization; albeit in the minor leagues. The fact that it was with a hometown team that just won the World Series made it even sweeter. My personal training career could wait — the White Sox definitely held top priority.

After signing the contract, I went to Grandstand, located just west of the ballpark on 35th Street, and bought my first White Sox hat. The 1976, navy blue throwback with white horizontal SOX block lettering was classic, and a perfect fit. Signing a contract not only got me back on the field; I had officially switched sides in Chicago's baseball war.

*   *   *   *

In this moment, being a walk-on or an undrafted free agent no longer mattered. At the Chicago White Sox spring training facility, in Tucson, Arizona, everyone was equal. No matter how we got there, or where we came from, we were all competing on the same baseball fields. There were players from across the United States, Canada, Latin America, and Asia. It was truly a global competition. Now was the real test. Some players might get more opportunities than others, but ultimately, performance mattered — not how much scholarship money you had, not what round you were drafted in, not what your signing bonus was (which was good for me because I didn't get a scholarship, wasn't drafted, and had no signing bonus). A good resume might get you on the field, but being able to stand and deliver was more important. *Do you really need a piece of paper to tell you you're the best?* My goal was to have an impressive spring training and break camp with a minor league team. I did not care where I ended up, only that I had earned a roster spot. I had zero expectation for how much I played; I was only concerned with making the most of any opportunity. Plus, I pledged to stand out by working so fucking hard that the White Sox had to keep me.

Throughout this journey, one of my regrets was not being

able to share special athletic moments with my family. They were supportive but never got to celebrate any real success. There was no Kent family exhilaration from signing a letter of intent to play for the Hawkeyes. There was no party when the Huskers advanced to the College World Series. There was no congratulations when I received the phone call from the MLB organization that drafted me. There was no campus invitation for Senior Day, to be proud of my Iowa Football or Nebraska Baseball career accomplishments. Because I hated Omaha, there was no graduation walk. I saw teammates in Iowa City and Lincoln, homegrown from their respective states, get teary-eyed the moment they saw their beloved hometown jersey hanging in their locker. With Hawkeyes or Huskers on the front, and their last name on the back, it was the pinnacle of pride. Having that connection was crucial to the program's identity, and as an out-of-state guy, I could only imagine what it felt like.

When I arrived at my locker and saw a black White Sox #14 jersey with KENT on the back, I understood everything. All the thrills that those Hawkeyes and Huskers felt now exploded through my body. The White Sox were my hometown team; Downers Grove was a 30-minute drive from Comiskey Park. Even now, I live in the Bridgeport neighborhood, just down the street from Guaranteed Rate Field. The South Side was even stronger on Juli's side of the family. The Marshaks lived in both the South Shore and Cottage Grove Heights neighborhoods. My grandfather, Irving, attended Hirsch High School; my Uncle John, Fenger High School; my Uncle Bill, South Shore High School. John played against NFL Hall of Famer and Chicago Bears icon Dick Butkus, who attended nearby Chicago Vocational High School. Before moving to Park Ridge in 1967, my mom and Aunt Pam went to Schmid School. They lived in the heart of the South Side and were all White Sox fans. Putting on the jersey was not just about me, it was about everyone that helped me sign this contract. Wearing the SOX on my chest was the most gratification I had felt since high school. I became emotional, but had to squash that shit real quick. The minor league clubhouse was filled with testosterone, and I was not about to be the new, old guy that cried on Day One. I'm not that kind of motherfucker. So, I took a few deep breaths, put on the uniform, found my Steve Trout-inspired confidence, and went to work.

*   *   *   *

In the NFL or NBA, once a player signs a contract they are immediately recognized as part of the team at the highest level of their sport. Baseball is completely different — no one travels from high school or college straight to the big leagues. Before getting to the majors, players must first succeed in the minors. The minor leagues have five different levels of development: Triple-A, Double-A, High-A, Low-A, and Rookie League. Usually, the more experienced players are at the higher levels while the newer ones begin their careers at the bottom. Everyone is grinding and fighting to move up. Players throughout the minor leagues have showcased a tool (or tools) that proves they belong in professional baseball. To be considered for a promotion, they have to consistently perform well over a large sample size against elevated competition. The ultimate promotion, which offsets the minor league stranglehold, is the dream of being called up to The Show.

I was assigned to the Low-A Kannapolis roster. Most Low-A players are in their early 20s, so Kannapolis was an odd place for an almost 28 year-old. But, no one in the White Sox organization had seen me play recently — possibly ever. All I could control was doing the work and seeing where it led me. John Orton, or J.O., was the White Sox minor league catching coordinator and in charge of all the catchers in the system. He was a great teacher, a great coach, and a great person — strongly reminding me of Aaron Nieckula. I confided in him that I had not played in two years, and asked him to point out any bad or lazy habits I may have accrued. I thought my offense might start slow, so I needed to lockdown my defense. Under J.O.'s watchful eye, I was ready for a great spring training.

When we finally started the spring training games, whether intra-squad scrimmages or against the Colorado Rockies and Arizona Diamondbacks, I figured I would not play much. Besides, I was a nobody and most likely the last guy on the roster. Imagine my surprise before our first intra-squad game, when J.O. told me I was in the starting lineup. I quickly had to control my adrenaline before it was time to show the White Sox what I could do. In my first live at-bat in two years, I crushed a ball to right center. When it left the bat, I was sure it was extra bases, possibly even a home run. *Holy shit*, I thought, *I got all of it*. But, speedy teenaged centerfielder

Kent Gerst ran it down at the wall for a long out. Clearly, I needed to adjust for a new kind of speed, a speed I had not seen in a few years: youth.

In the bottom of the first, Gerst got on base and tried to steal second. I threw him out. Shortly after, there was a play at home, where I had to block the plate, field a short-hop throw from the outfield, and apply the tag — all at the same time. It's one of the hardest asks of a catcher, but I made the play! In the first inning of my first game, after being off for two years, I made solid contact on offense, and was statistically responsible for two of the three outs on defense. Initial impressions were critical, especially for me, and it was the best start I could hope for. While everyone had ups and downs during spring training, I tried to carry myself like a champion and not get too high or too low. In the morning, I took the early bus to the park to do my strength training, and stayed after practice to work on my hitting. I caught any pitcher who wanted to throw and attempted to do everything in my power to make the White Sox keep me. Throughout camp, it was common for guys to get promoted, demoted, or released. Many players drove themselves crazy trying to anticipate the front office's next moves, over which they had zero control. The smartest, sanest option is to play hard, hustle hard, and let the cards fall where they may.

Toward the end of spring training, major leaguer catcher Toby Hall was thought to have suffered a season-ending shoulder injury, which created a ripple effect throughout the minor leagues. Hall was brought in as a free agent to backup fan favorite A.J. Pierzynski, and the loss was a big blow to the organization. The catchers, like chess pieces, were moved around, and J.O. said that I would bump up to Triple-A Charlotte. It was quite a promotion, as I skipped High-A Winston-Salem and Double-A Birmingham. Camp still had a week left, but for a guy who was out of baseball for two years, March had been a busy month. Now, I was getting a chance to play at the highest minor league level and my excitement was difficult to contain. Some of the White Sox's top prospects, like outfielders Ryan Sweeney and Jerry Owens and third baseman Josh Fields, were in Charlotte. The team was loaded with talent. With Charlotte, I played in one forgettable game against Arizona; a strikeout and a passed ball on my stat line — the definition of *NOT* taking advantage of an opportunity. Left-hander Shaun Babula threw a nasty cutter that bounced off my glove, my only passed ball of the spring. *Fuck me.*

At the end of camp, Charlotte played the major league Colorado Rockies in Tucson Electric Park. White Sox stars Jon Garland, Jim Thome, and Darin Erstad were my teammates. Todd Helton, the Rockies legend, was playing first base for Colorado. It was incredible to be in the same dugout with guys that for years, I had been watching on TV. In one month's time, I went from training 5am clients at Crunch, to Low-A Kannapolis, to Triple-A Charlotte, to wearing official, pinstriped White Sox pants for a major league spring training game! While I did not play in the game, I caught Garland in-between innings and truly believed anything was possible. My overall stats for the spring were a .250 average (5 for

20) while throwing out 7 of 12 base runners. *If I could just hit around .250 from the left side, my defensive skills might carry me to the next level.* They were solid numbers, but had I shown enough to justify keeping me around for the 2007 season?

*   *   *   *

In baseball, most players found out they were released by coming to their locker and seeing all their belongings in a black garbage bag (when I returned to clean out my locker in Lincoln, I was greeted by a big black Husker garbage bag). Every morning, instead of walking straight to my locker, I would peek around the corner and look for the garbage bag. I never saw one. But, the only way players knew they officially made a club was when the team athletic trainer confirmed it. On the last day of camp, no one had talked to me, so I was stuck in baseball purgatory. At some point, someone would explain my fate, and I wasn't sure if the news would be good. As the final practice ended and everyone left the field, a trainer found me with Charlotte and explained that I would be playing at the Low-A level, with the Kannapolis Intimidators. *Holy shit, I made it.* Now, and only now, I allowed myself a big smile and a bigger exhale. I was headed to Kannapolis, North Carolina to play in the South Atlantic League. I was probably too old to be there, but I actually made a team! I had *finally* achieved a baseball goal! Of course, I was numerous levels away from the major league White Sox, but after years of feeling like my stock was plummeting it was currently headed in the proper direction. I tried to play it cool with my emotions.

Many players were released those last few days — including my roommate, outfielder Tommy Paterson — and it's bad karma to outwardly celebrate in front of teammates that just received the worst news of their professional career.

Minutes later, J.O. intercepted me on my way back to the clubhouse. He told me that instead of heading to Kannapolis, I would be staying in Tucson for Extended Spring Training. Extended Spring Training is similar to the NFL's practice squad; players aren't on an official roster, but are worth holding onto. If anyone gets hurt, extended players are the insurance policy for every minor league team in the organization. Realisticially, extended would have been a good place for me. The more reps I had in practice, the better prepared I would be for the season. The downside was that if no one got hurt, I would be released before new players were brought in from the June amateur draft. But, if extended was my destination, I would do the best I could to stay ready. Plus, it was a good sign that the White Sox were keeping me around — at least two more months to impress them. I was willing to do the work on any field or in any town they placed me.

It was odd that, in a matter of minutes, I had been given two completely different baseball destinations — didn't they communicate internally? Either way, I was grateful to still be part of the White Sox organization. I knew I would only get better with repetition, so I was ready to work. Plus, as an older guy, I could show the younger players how to be professional and how to take care of their bodies. I would embrace my role as a leader and hope for the best. As I showered and changed clothes in the clubhouse — proud as hell of myself — word got to me that Alan Regier wanted to see me in his office. Alan was the director of player development, and one of the main voices throughout spring training. As a new player in the White Sox system, it was understandable that we should develop a relationship. I figured our introductory meeting was congratulatory and to discuss expectations.

However, Alan informed me that effective immediately, I was released from my contract. My career was over.

*   *   *   *

That last day of spring training was a whirlwind of emotions. In the span of 30 minutes, three different White Sox personnel gave me three different baseball destinations, each less appealing than the last. The final destination resulted in me catching a flight to Chicago, just not with the White Sox. Professional sports is a crazy business, but I am forever grateful to David Wilder and the Chicago White Sox. I did not achieve my goal of making a team, which was disappointing. But, I got the opportunity that had evaded me for years and I was in the best physical and mental condition to meet that opportunity. I left it all on the field and had zero regrets (except not making the team). My baseball career finally had closure. I also got to share Spring Training with my family. Jacque came for the first week. Terry and Uncle Bob came for the second week. My Aunt Pam, Uncle Tom, and cousin Willie drove from Southern California. My 84 year-old grandpa, Irving, came for the third week. Everyone got to see me play baseball in a Chicago White Sox uniform. This was better than Senior Day. They all knew how important baseball was to me, the sacrifices I made, and how hard I fought to get there. I was incredibly proud they all got to see it. While in Arizona, I talked to Bill Slight every day. I spoke with Garry Templeton, who reminded me that I had the talent to play at this level. I checked in with old Husker teammate Adam Stern, who was in big league camp with the Baltimore Orioles. Baseball united us, and it was amazing to reconnect with old friends.

Most White Sox fans will likely remember David Wilder, probably because of his stint in prison. In 2013, David pleaded guilty to skimming Latin American players on their signing bonuses. He may never work in baseball again, but I am truly grateful for our chance encounter and the opportunity he provided me. David handed over a contract to a player he never saw play; someone that he "scouted" out of a gym in downtown Chicago. He did not have to check with area scouts or a national cross-checker. David was a man of his word and did exactly what he said he would do — providing me with an extremely powerful life moment. It is an experience that I will always remember. Plus, I had no signing bonus, so I know he didn't steal any money from me.

Nike Training with Steph Rountree. Photo by Te Bates

REFLECTION

"SUCCESS IS A JOURNEY, NOT A DESTINATION.
HAVE FAITH IN YOUR ABILITY."

– Bruce Lee

This was a difficult story to write, as it was emotionally exhausting to relive the past. While I knew the ending, it still hurt to be reminded that I did not achieve my goal of becoming a Major League Baseball player. I did not make it to the big leagues. This book was never intended to be a "how to" guide or a "glory days" memoir. It was meant to demonstrate the power of grit and inner-strength because I advanced a lot further than I should have. Speaking of grit, Angela Duckworth, Ph.D, in her famous TED Talk defined grit as "a combination of passion and perseverance for a singularly important goal." I hope that current and future athletes will see the value of resiliency and the importance of embracing discipline to do the work under the best and worst of conditions.

In April, 2017, Joe Leccesi wrote an article for *USA Today* titled "The 5 Most Commonly Asked Questions About Being a College Walk-On." He explained the challenges of being a walk-on and ranks three tiers of walk-on hierarchy, all of which I experienced during my career. As an Iowa Football player, I was a *preferred walk-on* — the highest status of a walk-on. As an Iowa Baseball player, I was a *recruited walk-on* — defined as below preferred status but still having generated interest from the program. As a Nebraska Baseball player, I was an *unrecruited walk-on* — the lowest ranked tier; loosely defined as someone who just showed up. Coach Long had recruited me, Coach Broghamer had heard of me, and Coach Van Horn did not know me — all leading to drastically different experiences.

Leccesi explains that being a walk-on is not for everybody, as choosing to walk-on means choosing a more difficult athletic path than your scholarship teammates. He concludes the article by saying that "if you are an athlete who has had to grind for everything you have, are an excellent teammate, and are extra competitive (without harming your role as a team leader), you will probably have the character and work ethic needed to make it as a college walk-on." I agree with his assessment — a special mentality and discipline is required. Personally, I wanted to prove to myself that I belonged with the big boys, scholarship or no scholarship. Walking-on and earning respect will be an uphill battle, but one that is worth the climb. The best message of the article (and exactly what motivated me) is "when you do break through, success will be sweeter."

I would not recommend that anyone follow my path. Starting with choosing to play college football, I made some questionable career decisions. In addition, I thought I could play college baseball anywhere in the country; that my talent would be recognized by any coach on any field at any university. Talent is only part of the package. It is extremely helpful to be wanted within the program. Out of my three schools, only Iowa recruited me. Coach Long and Coach Banks were the only coaches in my college career who saw me play prior to my arrival. I had no history with Coach Broghamer, Coach Van Horn, or Coach Herold — this hurt our relationship. They did not bring me into their programs; I brought myself. In hindsight, it was a mistake to believe that I could walk-on and play my way onto their fields. My South coaches and Bill Slight knew me and understood my value. Coincidentally, I had my best success with them.

The time spent within a program had a direct effect on my success. I am the type of person who is extremely ethnocentric and has immense pride in his team, but after high school, I wasn't on any team for very long. I struggled in college, possibly because my college coaches all had me for less than two years (two football semesters in Iowa City, three baseball semesters each in Lincoln and Omaha). None of those three stops ever felt like "home." Comparatively, at South, Coach Belskis had me for two years; Coach Fox for three, and I developed into a two-sport Division I prospect. I played four summer baseball seasons for Bill Slight's Wheaton White Sox, equivalent to a "college experience." I was an MVP for him. Master Kim and Master Yoon had me for five years at Lions Martial Arts, and I earned my taekwondo black belt. I was at Crunch for five years, under James Bach, and became an elite level trainer. Sensei Douglas Tono had me for 11 years at Tohkon Judo Academy, and I earned my black belt. The more these coaches knew me, and understood me as a person, the better I performed.

Based on my effort, my experience should have had a different outcome. But, the tangible lesson is that effort alone does not guarantee victory.

*   *   *   *

Upon reflection, there were a couple of consistent themes in my college career. My two greatest off-the-field obstacles were mononucleosis and shoulder surgery. It's painful to admit, but they were both caused by the same factor: overtraining. The National Strength Coaches Association states that "overtraining syndrome can lead to dramatic performance decreases in all athletes; the most common cause is intensified training without adequate recovery." My obsession with improvement was detrimental in both circumstances. The summer before I reported to Iowa City, Terry told me (on many occasions) that I needed to slow down let my body recover. My stubborn 18 year-old self didn't listen.

Iowa Football was doomed the instant I got mono. A direct result of overtraining, "the kissing disease" immediately put me at a physical disadvantage. The summer of 1997 was packed with a chemistry class, baseball games, and football training. My nutrition was subpar, as I did not eat enough food, and I did not eat the right foods. I also did not sleep enough for adequate recovery. Ultimately, my football career ended because of it. To be an 183-pound fullback on a Big Ten roster was absurd. If I were going to seriously compete, I needed to gain about 50 pounds. In my life, I have never weighed more than 218 pounds, so any weight gained would have been forced and probably not sustainable. I understood that my body was not built for college football. The reality is that Big Ten football demands big bodies, and I was too small. If, as a freshman, I had been my normal 200 pounds, then the 20 pounds I gained in the offseason would have put me very close to what I wanted to weigh. It might have resulted in a different football story.

Iowa Baseball was doomed when Coach Banks retired. New coaches are not obligated to honor the arrangements of previous coaches. Like any business or organization, new leadership wants their own people in their system. I was a Coach-Banks-guy, not a Coach-Broghamer-guy. Unfortunately, Iowa became Broghamer's team, and I was not one of his recruits. Under Broghamer, Iowa Baseball had a .479 Big Ten winning percentage during my college years. In 2001, the Hawkeyes renamed their baseball facility Duane Banks Baseball Field. Coach Banks is the winningest coach in Iowa Baseball history. Timing is everything, and his dismissal was terrible timing for me.

Now at the University of Arkansas, Coach Van Horn has led both the Huskers and the Razorbacks to the College World Series. In 2018, he was one out away from winning it all and becoming an NCAA Division I National Champion. He has been the Big XII Coach of the Year, the SEC Coach of the Year, and the *Baseball America* National Coach of the Year. His resume is extremely impressive, and he has had a successful career coaching at major universities. Dave

Van Horn is a good, winning coach, one of the highest paid in college baseball. On paper, he is a coach I would want to play for. So, what happened in Lincoln? For years I tried to figure it out. I busted my ass for him, so why would a good, successful, winning college baseball coach not recognize and reward that? I was a coaches kid, a former Division I, Big Ten football player, and a future pro catcher. I would eventually sign with Garry Templeton and the Chicago White Sox organization. Why did he think that I did not belong? It made no sense. Although I showed significant improvement during my three semesters, he decided I was not part of his plans. Many times, players will reflect on their athletic career and question their commitment. *If I had worked harder; If I had taken it more seriously; If I had listened to my coaches...* I have mild satisfaction knowing there is nothing I would have done differently.

Coach Herold is Omaha's all-time winningest baseball coach. In years prior, he won two minor league championships with the Kansas City Royals organization. Like Van Horn, he has an extremely impressive coaching resume, and is a coach I would want to play for. Why didn't it work out for me? Probably because I got hurt. If there is anything I would do differently, it would be to take a break in the fall of 2000. That summer I caught every game — including doubleheaders — and it likely fatigued my arm, predisposing me to injury. I should have taken some time off to rest my body. But, Herold had only known me for one semester. I had not built up enough credibility and trust with him and felt like I needed to prove my worth. Asking for a break, after receiving a partial scholarship, was not the way to earn respect. I would have benefited from someone holding me back, because I could not do it myself. Did I have an awful 2001 season? Absolutely. But, I was also trying to play through a torn rotator cuff and attempting to save my college career from drowning in a big, shit-filled toilet bowl. Eliminating my scholarship after an injury that required major, career-threatening surgery was a huge kick in the balls; it felt like I had been discarded once no longer useful. Plus, the disconnect with the training staff during rehab left me emotionally drained. Omaha's Division II experience fell far short of my expectations, but my college baseball career ended because of overuse.

It is essential that all athletes understand the balance between work and recovery.

* * * *

Sports, like life, will constantly test our grit. How we handle adversity is what defines our character. Success is determined by our resilience. There were many moments in which it would have been easy to tap out and quit the game. Niketown Chicago has one of my favorite Michael Jordan quotes painted on a second floor wall, right by the escalators: *If you quit once it becomes a habit. Never quit.* At South, I could have quit when I wasn't drafted or offered a scholarship. In Iowa City, I could have quit when I was diagnosed with mono or when Broghamer cut me. In Lincoln, I could have quit when Van Horn tore me up in back-to-back meetings. In Omaha, I could have quit when Herold yanked my scholarship or after I had shoulder surgery. In the independent leagues, I could have quit when I was released from Schaumburg, Gary, Joliet, and San Angelo. I could have quit when I started personal training at Crunch. But, that's not me — I am not a quitter.

I got knocked down — figuratively and literally — too many times to count. Each time, a strong self-belief powered me to stand back up. I knew I could play Division I football and baseball. I also knew I could play baseball professionally. It is important to note that believing something is true does not make it true. Just because I *believe* I'm a superhero, does not mean *I am* a superhero. I have to do that superhero work to earn superhero status, which is why I put countless hours into strengthening my mental and physical game. I needed to know that my training and my commitment was greater than my competition. Throughout my career, I found peace in knowing that I worked as hard as I knew how, with years devoted to training my weaknesses. Most people concentrate on their strengths, because it reminds them why they're good. The real pros will work their asses off in areas of weakness. Practice does not make perfect; perfect practice makes perfect.

Many books have been written about the benefits of deliberate practice, the only true way to strengthen weaknesses. It is essential to dedicate self-practice time to work on the worst possible situations; the hardest parts of your game. I always blocked balls in the dirt, going through buckets of baseballs to get it right. I would create a real-life scenario: *Bottom of the ninth, tying run on third; need to smother this 1-2 slider.* If any ball got past me, I'd do it again. At the Bulls/Sox Training Academy, I used to sit close to the pitching machine, and work on catching super-fast fastballs. In the batting cage, I practiced hitting with two strikes. In the gym, I did one-legged squats because they were hard for me. I ran the 300-yard shuttle because I hated it. I was willing to trade practice misery for game success.

The classic movie *Rudy* is a great feel-good sports story, but no one wants to be Rudy. No one wants to be the little guy that has the will but not the size. While I was definitely too small for Iowa Football, my body was just fine for college and pro baseball. The goal of my training was always to be the best player I could be, to be stronger and faster while improving all areas of weakness. At 6'2" and 210 pounds, I had the physical traits to pass the eyeball test. With a pop time under 2.0, I had the necessary arm strength to be a pro catcher. As a left-handed hitter, I had the timing to consistently put the bat on the ball. As a college football player, I had the mentality to run through a wall for my team. What I didn't have, outside of Bill Slight, was the opportunity to show it on a regular basis. If I was 5'6" 140 pounds, with a pop time of 2.5 seconds, no amount of self-belief would make up for a lack of physical talent. My physicality reinforced my belief, which added to my confidence: I can do this.

Making it to the big leagues would have been the ultimate finale to this story, but this is not a Disney fairy tale. I didn't make it; there was no happy ending to my baseball career. On the last day of spring training, I was told that I made the Kannapolis team. Then I was told I was staying in Tucson. Then I was told I was going home. Just like that, my employment with the Chicago White Sox was over. It was the last time I would ever put on a baseball uniform, with the Cactus League as the final destination on my baseball timeline. Looking back on it now, sometimes the journey is more important than the outcome. If I had been with the White Sox as a 20 year-old, then would I have appreciated it as much? Would I have worked as hard? To paraphrase Teddy Roosevelt, I did the best I could, with what I had, where I was. The White Sox rewarded my endurance, even though it was not the result I hoped for. At some point, most athletes will experience a gut-check; a time to demonstrate how important it is to reach a goal. In an era that lacks patience, staying true to the cause is an important lesson. Some people want to achieve, but only when it's convenient or easy. Today, we can push a button on our phone and be rewarded with instant gratification. How bad would you want it if you had to wait *years* to get it?

My hope is that everyone who reads this book stays inspired and committed to accomplish a goal, regardless of the timeline. Whatever you're after, do the work to get the result. If I can do it, you can do it. Take advantage of opportunities. Be disciplined. Be a leader. Have strong character and conviction. Like Nike said, just do it.

*   *   *   *

3 TIPS FOR ATHLETES

1. Have an Honest Talent Assessment

The job of parents is to tell their kids how great they are. The job of coaches, by contrast, is to accurately assess talent and evaluate potential. If your goal is to be a high level athlete, then a neutral party needs to identify your strengths and weaknesses. Everything will be judged, especially physical characteristics: Height, weight, speed, natural ability, desire. Once your talent has been scrutinized, then it will be compared to other prospects, both locally and nationally (and in some cases, internationally). Being the best player in your town is nice, but plenty of high school studs don't pan out because the quality of competition keeps evolving.

Find ways to separate yourself by understanding your own strengths and weaknesses. If you're a 6'5" and 290lb defensive tackle, find out if you have good technique or you're just good at being 6'5" and 290lbs. The size/speed advantage in high school gets nullified as the competition increases because at the top levels, everyone is big and fast. You actually need to have skill.

2. Be Committed

Are you 6'9" with a 98-mph fastball, a 50-inch vertical jump, a 4.21 40-yard dash, and a 1.0 GPA? For college the only number that matters is your GPA. Bad grades disqualify you from opportunities. The academic reality is that you need to apply yourself the same way as you do on the field. Your commitment to the classroom is important to secure a future post-career.

Speaking of commitments, college sports are a huge time-consumer. Expect to make personal and social sacrifices. Depending on the sport, you may be required to stay on campus in the summer to train for the upcoming season. While your non-athlete friends are on vacation doing tequila shots, you'll be running stadium steps at 6am. Get used to it.

3. Handle Criticism Well

College coaches keep their jobs by winning; by trusting their professional careers to the brains and bodies of 18 to 23 year-olds. They are under immense pressure and stress. Most coaches can be a bit salty when evaluating performance, and there is a strong chance you will be criticized. For some athletes, it's the first time they've heard such a message. Developing emotional resilience is important, as you will need a short memory to mentally survive.

If you can be coachable, and understand what is being said, instead of how it's being said, your ability to handle criticism should improve. Don't take it personally, even when it is personal. Remember that everyone has an opinion, so keep a tight circle of influence. Keep perspective and carry yourself like a champion.

3 TIPS FOR COACHES

1. Know Your Players

This should be a no-brainer. You picked these kids for your program; it's your job to know them as people. Understand how they're motivated and how they respond to certain coaching styles. Some kids are hard enough on themselves, so back off. Others are not hard enough, so it's time to light a fire. Take the time to develop rapport with your players, their families, and their previous coaches. It might be worth a couple wins now, and a couple players in the future.

2. Be a Leader

Leaders don't just talk about it, they are about it. They need to act as if they live the virtues of their program. Players will follow someone who fights for them, who allows them to fail without embarrassment. Stand up for your athletes; you might be the only person in their lives who does.

The game is hard enough, so a positive culture is a must. Remember that mistakes will happen and reinforce playing aggressive instead of playing scared. How we do anything is how we do everything, and it all starts at the top with the head coach. Always lead by example.

3. Have Fun

The reason kids pick up a ball is that the game is fun. If the game wasn't fun, no one would play. As the athletes elevate to higher levels, more stress is involved, and fun is often forgotten. The best coaches remember to keep the game fun.

Joe Maddon perfected this tactic throughout his stint managing the Cubs. From pajama onesies to Miami Vice-themed suits, he has emphasized "fun" during a monotonous 162-game schedule. The players appreciate the team bonding aspect, and seeing Joe and his staff participate strengthens their credibility.

Laughing at yourself and not taking yourself too seriously are key components to succeeding at the top. Remember to have fun.

3 TIPS FOR TRAINERS

1. Do The Work

The best way to be recognized as a top trainer is to actually train people. Too often, I see trainers putting all of their energy into their social media accounts, and not enough time into building their business. Is social media important? Maybe. But, having a booked schedule is way more impressive than any Instagram post.

Unless you are consistently training 120 or more hours per month, you do not have a full schedule. Set goals for two to three clients in the early morning, two to three clients in the afternoon, and two to three clients in the evening. Or book yourself with eight straight hours. The more you train the more money you make, so start turning relationships into clients.

2. Improve Yourself

The human body is amazing, and there is always more to learn about what it can do. No one knows everything (and be wary of someone who thinks they do) so there are many areas for improvement. Ask yourself what your weaknesses are, and add a certification to strengthen them. Learn more about boxing, pilates, yoga, Olympic lifting, etc. Taking the time to add to your knowledge base introduces you to different audiences, which is always good for business.

In addition, it's important to test yourself. Sign up for a marathon. Compete in the Golden Gloves Tournament. Run a 5K turkey trot. Find something to hold you accountable to a training program, which might help you relate to your clients.

3. Look Professional

Let's face it: Wearing Nike sweatpants to work is awesome. While the fitness industry is already pretty lax on its dress code, separate from the competition by holding yourself to a higher standard. Find a style that works for you, and while your biceps might be bigger than the Sears Tower, your sweaty armpit hair might turn off potential (or current) clients. Also, is that skimpy tank top showing off your ripped pecs? Sweet. Remember this: No one in the gym wants to see your nipples. Be a pro, bro.

This is a hot and sweaty job, so keep good hygiene. We work in close proximity with human bodies all day long, so personal cleanliness is incredibly important. Be conscious of anywhere odors can escape — it's okay for clients to stink; it's not okay for trainers.

Inside the huddle with David Carson, Gina Gaifano and the Nike Chicago team. Photo by Emmanuel Camacho

CONCLUSION

"TOUGH TIMES DON'T LAST, TOUGH PEOPLE DO."
– Mike Ditka

I had a choice regarding how these experiences would shape my future, especially outside of baseball. It would have been easy to become a bitter, resentful person and feel sorry for myself because college was difficult for me. But, I am not a person that chooses easy. The universe was constantly challenging my character to see what path I would choose. While those college years were tough, I always felt like my best days were in front of me.

When Crunch closed in 2008, I took my personal training business private to work for myself as an independent contractor, BKSTRENGTH, LLC. In an industry where the average career lasts three to four years, I have consistently evolved my product, increased my education, and tried to produce an excellent training experience. Not all clients can do everything I want them to, so like any good teacher, I learned how to make modifications in real-time. I had a great example to follow regarding the importance of adjusting teaching styles. At South, Terry taught advanced placement calculus to students who were valedictorians; and fundamentals of geometry to kids who were lucky to graduate high school. He taught kids that were great at math, and ones that were not (I took geometry twice, so I'm allowed to say that). An important point, that showed Terry's value as a teacher, was his ability to equally reach two drastically different audiences. It's easy to teach kids who understand the material; it's much harder to teach kids who take longer to "get it."

I have tried to follow Terry's blueprint with my clients. All personal trainers have a similar knowledge base. We all know the same movement patterns and the same exercises. The difference is how we apply our knowledge. Not every exercise is right for every client, and a true professional can differentiate between what is appropriate for each individual. I have tried to create a program that helps clients move better and feel better. My goal is not to break people down, but to help them improve weaknesses. I also want them to understand the process, so they leave feeling educated and empowered. Much like Lacey Degnan in Lincoln, we have fun and laugh while getting our work in.

My clientele is extremely diverse. I have worked with everyone from athletes (pro, college and high school baseball players; Olympic judoka; college and high school wrestlers; MMA fighters; boxers; college and high school volleyball players) to senior citizens. Obviously, they do not train the same way. There are ideas that crossover, but knowing each person's strengths and weaknesses and effectively communicating our goals is crucial for building trust and credibility. If I train a cage-fighter like a grandmother, then I'm an idiot. If I train a grandmother like a cage-fighter, then I'm also an idiot (unless I had a cage-fighting grandmother — that would be awesome). But, I should be able to help both the cage-fighter and the grandmother perform better — however we have agreed to define it.

It seems like the industry has trended toward putting people through brutal, ass-kicking workouts. While there is a place for higher intensity training, most people don't have the fitness base to handle such a workload. The truth is that due to an "office lifestyle," most adults don't move well. If people don't move their own bodies well, then they sure as hell won't move well with an external load. As trainers, it is important that we think independently and ask ourselves, "is this exercise good for this person?" Do all humans need to train for repetitive triple extension power? Should 18 year-olds and 45 year-olds train the same way? Only you can decide.

*   *   *   *

In 2015, Nike asked me to be a trainer for their Train Chicago project. I have always loved Nike and was thrilled about this opportunity. The Train Chicago facility was just east of the United Center; a West Side warehouse turned into an athlete training mecca. It looked like a modern, Nike version of Husker Power. Train Chicago was a sport-specific training experience, with each workout week aligning to a different sport and corresponding Nike athlete: Special teams ace Sherrick McMannis of the Bears; Stanley Cup winner Trevor van Riemsdyk of the Blackhawks; goalie Sean Johnson of the USMNT and Fire; future World Series champion Anthony Rizzo and strength coach Tim Buss of the Cubs; and six-time NBA champion and Bulls legend Scottie Pippen. Nike brought out A-list talent, putting Chicago at the center of the training universe. Train Chicago concluded with an all-encompassing total athlete workout and appearance from Bo Jackson. Bo was my two-sport hero, and I wore #8 on the South freshman baseball team because it was Bo's White Sox jersey number. I was fortunate enough to shake his hand; Bo Knows strong handshakes.

Like in high school, making the most of an opportunity lead to more opportunities. Train Chicago has morphed into multiple Nike projects: Train Chicago 2.0, Get Out Here, Nike Detroit, Swoosh Saturday, Nike Training Club, and MetCon Monday. I even had an opportunity to work on a #BeTrue campaign photo shoot with athletes Chris Mosier and Scout Bassett, which was filmed at McCormick Place. When Nike Chicago restructured their training roster I "made the team" and signed my first of a handful of Nike contracts, creating professional gratification equivalent to my White Sox contract. It has been a truly amazing experience, and as a veteran trainer, solidifies the importance of doing the work. The universe rewards those that put in the time to perfect their craft.

Shortly after, I partnered with my longtime friend Emily Hutchins, to take BKSTRENGTH into On Your Mark Coaching and Training. Emily has owned OYM since 2007, its original location was in the West Loop. As a Nike Master Trainer, she has had great success training clients, teaching classes, and coaching endurance athletes. As a trainer, I preferred one-on-ones and never taught any group classes. Emily allowed me the freedom to design and program three of my own classes — Ninja, Ballers, and Youth Athletic Conditioning — before asking me to become her director of performance and part of the OYM leadership council. In 2018, OYM opened its newest location, West Side, in the East Garfield Park neighborhood. It's a 7,000 square foot sports performance training center, and the emphasis of this beautiful facility is on youth sports and team training. We created a "big league atmosphere" for Chicago athletes. Come train with us!

I am building toward having a greater role within team sports. With OYM West Side, we now have a facility to house young athletes. There is nothing in Chicago like it. Whether it be through strength and conditioning or sport-specific coaching, the next phase of my career will be on the field or on the mat somewhere. Recently, I have worked with judo, track, volleyball, soccer, and baseball club programs. With my experiences as a player, I have witnessed the differences between good and bad leadership. All great coaches display accountability by explaining how the game is greater than wins and losses, and create a culture that facilitates success on the field and in life. My clients have benefited from this philosophy for many years, so it's a perfect transition.

Wherever life takes me, the best version of myself will be ready.

With Jacque and Raleigh at Maggie's wedding; October 2020.
Photo by Nicole Jansma

ACKNOWLEDGMENTS

The best part about Nebraska was meeting Jacque. She was an eyewitness and lived through most of this book. When I transferred from Lincoln to Omaha, I briefly moved into the Glynn's basement and was fortunate to have Jacque's family as my local support team. Even though we were both 19 years-old, I immediately realized that there was something different about her. Jacque was equivalently motivated to succeed and held herself to a high standard; unlike anyone I had ever known. She was beautiful, talented, driven, and disciplined. We also had similar athletic fates. A two-year veteran of the Scarlet Dance Team, Jacque was cut when she tried out for year three — along with a handful of teammates. Devastated at first, she channeled her focus and energy into interior design, studying in both San Francisco and London. The early part of our relationship was impacted by baseball's many uncertainties and physical distance. Somehow, we stayed together and were married in 2008. I am grateful to have shared these experiences with her — thank you for believing in me.

This project started in November 2017, and after 23 rounds of full-book edits, was finished in November 2020. During a normal work schedule, I spend the majority of my time in the gym with clients and teams, so finding the mental capacity to squeeze in proofreading, editing, and listening to myself read it aloud was challenging. I am not a professional writer and do not have a designated place to write. My iMac computer sits atop our kitchen island — which moonlights as a station to do homework or to play with Legos. I'm sure that Jacque and our daughter, Raleigh, are tired of me mentally isolating myself while physically being in the same room, as I have a gift (or curse) of eliminating distractions and focusing completely on whatever I'm doing. I apologize for sacrificing our family time — thank you for your patience.

Of course, I could not successfully complete this project alone.

My sister, Maggie Kent, was able to (1) remotely project manage me from Nashville, Tennessee; and (2) overcome all of my computer incompetencies as well as format the entire book. I wrote the content, but she created everything else. All of this was accomplished while running her full-time graphic design studio, Hello Gypsy. In addition to her design career, getting married, and buying a home, she still masterfully organized and styled this book. Her commitment from start to finish rivaled my own, and Maggie's vision led this book from its infancy to the polished product you have in your hands now. Thank you for bringing *Walked On* to life.

The cover art was created by Portland resident and Nike designer, Jason Wright. My colleagues at Nike Chicago introduced me to Jason when he was in town for SoxFest 2020. After drinks at Cork & Kerry and dinner at Franco's Ristorante, I was impressed with his passion, preparation, and attention to detail. He was the perfect addition to the book's presentation, and spoke the same design language as Jacque and Maggie. I am proud to have his talent on display — thank you.

My aunt, Pam Marshak, has worked in the newspaper business for 30 years in New York, Virginia, Florida, and California. Her expertise as an editor was extremely helpful in cleaning up my sentence structure and improving my word choices. After she confided that "no one knows how to write anymore," I was nervous that I could be in the same category. I feared that she would shred the entire book, leaving me to question my writing ability. To my surprise, Pam liked what she read and was instrumental in this project's completion, which gave me the confidence that various audiences might be interested in reading this. Thank you for injecting me with positive energy.

A longtime client/friend, Bill Bietsch has double master's degrees and craves education in ways that very few adults do. During our conversations, he enjoys using words that I have never heard before and takes immense pride in his vast vocabulary. Skilled at writing and verbal judo, Bill's thesaurus-like brain was extremely helpful in the early stages of editing and providing suggestions to add more in-depth details to the content. Each chapter is stronger because of his guidance. Thank you for challenging me.

For everyone who provided written endorsements, it takes guts to attach your name next to mine, especially since many of you agreed to help without knowing the full capacity of *Walked On*. I truly respect the credibility that you have earned on and off the field. Thank you, Coach Belskis. Thank you, Coach Fox. Thank you, Tony Williams. Thank you, Julianne Sitch. Thank you, Emily Hutchins. Thank you, Doug Tono. Thank you, Jennifer Nijman and Steven Surdell. Thank you, Ryan Curry. Thank you, Ken Harvey. I am proud to be aligned with such an incredibly talented group of people. Iron sharpens iron and this book is stronger because of you; I am stronger because of you.

Last, but not least, my parents, Juli and Terry, and sister, Ally. Over the years our family garage has been transformed into an unrecognizable storage unit. But, buried in all that chaos were tokens of credibility — the photos that help add physical placement to each chapter, as well as the letter to my teammates that had segments inserted into the LINCOLN chapter. The Kents were just as frustrated as I was during this journey — if not more — and could only watch from the sidelines while my pursuits drove me across the United States. Thank you for always believing in me and for encouraging me to write *Walked On*.

*   *   *   *

A portion of *Walked On*'s book sales have been donated to the On Your Mark Coaching and Training Game Changers scholarship fund — thank you for contributing. Led by Nike Master Trainer and OYM leadership council member David Carson, Game Changers is an athletic training program designed to give Chicago's youth the building blocks of performance and development.

The scholarship awards qualified young athletes access to a high-level training experience, which will service the athlete both on and off the field. To learn more, donate, or train with us, visit oymtraining.com.

ABOUT THE AUTHOR

Brian Kent is a Chicago-based personal trainer, the owner of BKSTRENGTH, part of the leadership council at On Your Mark Coaching and Training, and a Nike trainer. Before becoming a trainer, Kent was a two-sport Division I collegiate athlete and minor league baseball player. A lifelong martial artist, he has earned black belts in taekwondo and judo. Learn more at bkstrength.com and @bkstrength_chicago.

Photo by Bianca Garcia

Made in the USA
Monee, IL
03 January 2021